CONTENTS

C000319803

Gymnastic Activities in the NC _____ 4

Apparatus work _____ 4

Reception Year lessons and notes_____ 6

Year 1 lessons and notes _____28

Year 2 lessons and notes _____50

Index _____72

Gymnastic Activities in the NC

(1) A dual emphasis: performing and learning
• **Planning**: we challenge pupils to plan and respond thoughtfully.
• **Performing**: we encourage pupils to work hard in a focused way.
• **Reflecting and evaluating**: we assist pupils to progress as they adapt, change and plan again, guided by their own and others' judgements and comments after a performance.

(2) Required activities: KS1 PoS
Pupils should be taught:
(a) different ways of travelling on hands and feet, rolling, jumping, balancing, swinging, climbing and turning on floor and apparatus
(b) how to link together a series of actions, both on floor and using apparatus, and how to repeat them.

(3) Attainment Target: End of KS Descriptions
Pupils should be able to demonstrate that they can:
(a) plan and perform simple skills safely
(b) show control in linking simple actions together
(c) practise to improve performance, alone and with others
(d) describe what they and others are doing, and reflect on and make simple judgements about performances
(e) recognise the changes happening to the body during exercise.

(4) 'Good practice': General Requirements for all KSs
Pupils should be taught to:
(a) respond readily to instructions
(b) work hard physically and be helped to develop suppleness, strength and stamina, and a healthy heart and lungs
(c) try hard to make and maintain improvement
(d) be considerate towards others
(e) lift, carry, place and use equipment safely
(f) wear appropriate clothing and be aware of the safety risks of inappropriate clothing, footwear and jewellery.

(5) Assessing pupils' achievement
Three headings summarise the areas within which we want our pupils to achieve, in NC terms.
• **Performing** successfully is the main aim, demonstrating well-controlled, neat, accurate, varied, wholehearted work, and sharing the space unselfishly with a concern for own and others' safety.
• **Planning** and thinking ahead precede the performance, ideally demonstrating good understanding; sensible, safe decisions; and a willingness to listen to and adapt to others' views.
• **Evaluating and reflecting** and helpful, positive comments by oneself, the teacher or others, after a performance, help to inspire and guide pupils as they alter, develop and improve their work.

Apparatus work

One of the NC requirements is that pupils should be taught how to lift, carry, place and use equipment safely. To assist this it is recommended that the portable apparatus is placed at the sides or ends of the hall, adjacent to where it will be used in the lessons. By only having to lift and carry a short, 2–3 metre distance, the groups of five or six pupils need very little time to lift ('One at each end, one at each side, bend your knees and lift.') their apparatus safely.

At the end of the apparatus work, pupils return to their starting apparatus places to put away the apparatus they brought out. This leaves the floor clear for the incoming class and its floorwork.

FIXED AND PORTABLE APPARATUS

Apparatus referred to in the lesson plans that follow, and shown in the examples of simple and larger apparatus groupings, include the following items.

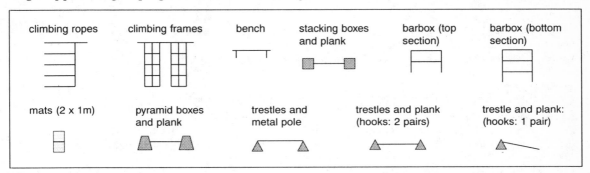

Minimum number recommended
- 12 x mats (2 x 1m).
- 3 x benches.
- 1 x barbox which can be divided into two smaller boxes by lifting off the top section. The lower section should have a platform top.
- 1 x pair stacking boxes, 19 x 19in (48 x 48cm) base, 13in (33cm) high; and one 8ft (2.4m) plank.

- 1 x pair pyramid boxes, 31in (78cm) high, 24in (60cm) long, 21in (53cm) wide at base tapering to 15in (38cm) wide at top, and one 8ft (2.4m) plank.
- 1 x pair of 3ft (1m), 3.5ft (1.06m), 4.6ft (1.4m) trestles.
- 2 x planks with two pairs of hooks.
- 2 x planks with one pair of hooks.
- 1 x 10ft (3m) metal pole.

EXAMPLES OF APPARATUS LAYOUTS

simple layout

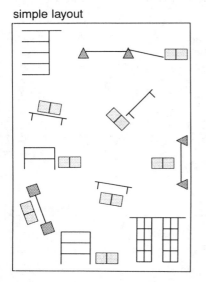

simple layout

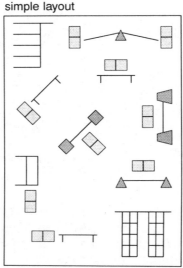

larger groups layout

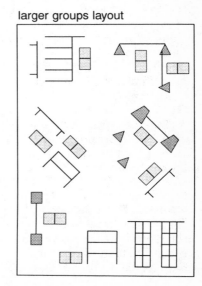

LESSON PLAN • 30 MINUTES

Emphasis on: (a) creating a quiet, industrious atmosphere with good responses to instruction; (b) good use of the feet in travelling and jumping, sharing the limited space safely; (c) co-operating with others to lift, carry and place the simple apparatus quietly, safely and sensibly.

FLOORWORK   12 minutes

Legs
(1) Walk, using all the floor space, going in and out of one another.
(2) When I call 'Stop!', show me how quickly you can find a space, all by yourself, not near anyone else. 'Stop!'
(3) Let your arms swing as you walk, visiting all parts of the room where you can see a space.
(4) Change to quiet running now. Can you go to the corners, the sides, ends and sometimes the middle of the room?
(5) When I call 'Stop!', show me a lovely, running body shape, in your own space. 'Stop!'

Legs and body
(1) Stay where you are, in your good space, and show me a big jump up and a nice, squashy landing.
(2) Push the floor hard with both feet and feel your ankles stretching.
(3) Really swing up with both arms to help your big jump. Let both arms swing backwards, then forwards, and right up above your head.
(4) In your landing, can you let your knees bend for a nice, soft, squashy finish?

APPARATUS WORK   16 minutes

(1) Walk all round the room, but do not touch the apparatus yet. You may go under, over, along or in and out of the pieces, but do not touch them.
(2) When I call 'Stop!' , stop on the nearest piece of apparatus and really stretch up high to the ceiling. 'Stop!'
(3) Now jump off with a nice, squashy landing on the floor, and off you go, walking, running or skipping in and out again. Are you going to all parts of the room, keeping well away from the other children? 'Stop!'

(4) You may now go on to the apparatus with a step or a jump, then jump down again, with your nice, squashy, quiet landing. Move to a different piece of apparatus.
(5) I am looking at the ways you travel between apparatus. Please show me your very best walking, running, skipping or even bouncing. I am looking for beautifully neat feet and legs as you travel.
(6) Can you show me a nicely stretched body as you jump from your apparatus, and then your squashy landing?

FINAL FLOOR ACTIVITY   2 minutes

Can you show me a way or ways to travel to all parts of the room, going in and out of one another? (Look out for and comment on neat examples of walking, running, skipping, hopping, bouncing with feet apart or together and slipping sideways.)

FLOORWORK

Legs

(1) Young primary school pupils will all follow one another in an anti-clockwise circle unless taught to do otherwise. We want them to 'Walk on straight lines, not curving, following others.'

(2) This is an exercise in listening for and giving an instant response to an instruction, namely to 'Stop!' Be firm with non-responders because they are time-wasting, diminishing the amount of time for activity and the enjoyment of the lesson.

(3) Pursue 'good' movement, even in something as natural as walking. Good posture and smart, brisk walking, with praise where it is deserved, sets a standard of hard-working, vigorous effort for this and subsequent lessons.

(4) Good, quiet running is marked by a good lifting in heels, knees and arms. Once again, they will tend to circle anti-clockwise, and they must be reminded 'Run straight, all by yourself.'

(5) The exercise in responding asks for an immediate stop and an inclined body in a good running position, one leg and one arm forwards.

Legs and body

(1) Ensure that all are well spaced for the jumping, away from other children and all the surrounding apparatus.

(2) A teacher demonstration of the push from balls of feet and the stretch of the ankle joint is recommended.

(3) A slow, long arm swing starts behind you and goes up to a full stretch above head. Many of our physical activities can be assisted by a preliminary swing of the arms.

(4) A teacher demonstration of the meaning of 'nice, squashy landing' is recommended until members of the class themselves can be asked to show the 'give' in knees and ankles for the safe, soft finish.

APPARATUS WORK

The simple apparatus has been placed round the sides and ends of the room, next to where it will be positioned. The pupils are grouped in fours and seated on the floor beside their piece – 'Our number one apparatus'. The apparatus is brought out slowly and carefully and put in position by one group at a time, guided and assisted by the teacher. The four children go 'one at each end and one at each side' for the benches, barbox top and bottom, stacking boxes and plank. Mats are carried by two children.

(1) Encourage brisk walking on the floor, without touching any apparatus. A teacher demonstration will explain 'over; under; in and out.' 'Along' can be astride a bench, for

example.

(2) On 'Stop!' respond immediately on nearest piece of apparatus. Be perfectly still, stretched tall with arms reaching up.

(3) The careful jump off uses the correct, 'giving' landing practised in the floorwork. We now encourage greater variety in the methods of travelling around apparatus.

(4) Apparatus is now to be used freely, on and off, non-stop.

(5) Look out for, praise and demonstrate examples of good quality and variety in the travelling on the floor.

(6) The firm, stretched body in flight contrasts with the soft, 'giving' body on landing.

FINAL FLOOR ACTIVITY

Ask them to show their 'favourite way or ways to travel to all parts of the hall, performed beautifully.'

Reception Year • October • Lesson 2

LESSON PLAN • 30 MINUTES

Emphasis on: (a) experiencing enjoyment and excitement through participation in varied physical activity; (b) enjoying the unselfish co-operation of everyone in sharing the floor and apparatus space; (c) practising and learning varied, well controlled ways of travelling on feet and on feet and hands; (d) establishing the tradition of lifting, carrying, placing and using apparatus quietly, safely and sensibly.

FLOORWORK   12 minutes

Legs

(1) Walk and run, quietly, in and out of one another, and visit every part of the room.

(2) Can you go to the sides, corners, ends and sometimes through the middle of the room?

(3) When I call 'Stop!', show me a big, high jump and a squashy landing in a space all by yourself. 'Stop!' (Repeat.)

(4) Now, show me some other way or ways that you can travel, using your feet only. (Look out for and comment on hopping, skipping, galloping, bouncing.)

Body

(1) Can you run one or two steps into a space near you, jump up high and then do a squashy landing? Then stand up, look for another space, and off you go again.

(2) Can you help your good landings by holding your arms out forwards or sideways to help your balance?

(3) Your squashy landings will be even quieter if you land on your toes and then let your knees bend a little bit.

Arms

(1) Can you travel about the hall using hands and feet only?

(2) Travel very slowly (not scampering) and help yourself by keeping away from all the others.

(3) Keep your arms nice and straight as you move them, and point your fingers forwards.

APPARATUS WORK   16 minutes

(1) Walk all round the room without touching any apparatus. You can go under, over, across, in and out of, and around the pieces, but don't touch any yet.

(2) Now change to your own favourite ways to travel on the floor, still not touching apparatus. You might jump across part of a mat; step over a bench; crawl under a plank; creep through a space in the climbing frame; or bounce along, astride a bench.

(3) Now using your feet only, can you show me ways of getting on to, travelling along, and then

coming off the apparatus? Remember 'Feet only. No hands!'

(4) Change now to using your hands and feet to help you on to the apparatus, and travel across or along it.

(5) I would be very pleased to see you come on to the apparatus using your hands strongly in some way. (Look out for and comment on twists, levers, pulls and bunny jumps on.)

(6) I would like to see you leave some pieces of apparatus with a nice, stretched jump and a soft, squashy landing on your mat.

FINAL FLOOR ACTIVITY   2 minutes

Follow me, all walking... jogging... skipping... bouncing... hopping... and now anything you like doing.

FLOORWORK

Legs

(1) Running quietly is helped by feeling a lifting in your heels and knees. The noisy, flat-footed style often seen (and heard) is quickly improved by some demonstrations.

(2) The teacher can join in and show 'I am visiting the corner..., now the side..., now the middle..., now one end..., and I am not following anyone...' This illustrates most clearly what is wanted when pupils travel about, sharing a small space.

(3) For the sake of a virtually unimpeded, full and busy lesson, the immediate response must become a tradition in this and all physical education lessons.

(4) Variety; trying out and learning new skills; individuality; and extending the teacher's and the class' repertoire, are all being pursued here.

Body

(1) One or two steps only, so that the jumping and landing are the main things. Restrain those who run all round the room before doing their jump. Tell them that you are looking at their eyes to see if they are really looking around for the next space to run to.

(2) A teacher demonstration of the meaning of 'straight arms helping the balanced landing' will illustrate this good point.

(3) A demonstration with half the class watching the other half can have the challenge 'Look out for and tell me who is landing on their toes, with knees bending a little bit.'

Arms

(1) Most will start crawling forwards far too quickly for it to have any beneficial physical effects. Slow, careful, deliberate travel on hands and feet, particularly when transferred to apparatus, is what we are looking for.

(2) Ask them to 'Look out for and travel into good spaces again' to counter the usual massing in the centre of the floor.

(3) Straight arms are strong, safe arms, particularly when we move on to inverting and supporting the whole body on hands alone.

APPARATUS WORK

(1) While the class are walking, using floor only, the teacher can do any last minute adjustments to the apparatus placement.

(2) Planning is called for to negotiate each piece of apparatus. Use appropriate actions, still not touching apparatus.

(3) Now there's the fun of going on to, moving along, and then coming off the apparatus, but only using feet at this stage. Mostly they will be stepping or jumping on and off, non-stop. Encourage them not to queue – another important tradition to establish.

(4) Using hands and feet enables them to travel everywhere, including on the climbing frames where they were not able to work using feet only.

(5) When coming on to climbing frames, demonstrate the correct, safe, 'thumbs under' position. When weight is all on hands, ask for straight arms, as when coming on to or crossing a bench.

(6) While the hands are important in helping you on, the feet will be important in helping you from the apparatus. The jumps off are exhilarating to young pupils, and we want them to be safe in their landings.

FINAL FLOOR ACTIVITY

Lively; varied; teacher's choice; our choice.

LESSON PLAN • 30 MINUTES

Emphasis on: (a) planning and performing simple skills safely; (b) body shape awareness, both in held positions, such as a balance, and in travelling; and in working hard to show a neat, firm body shape to enhance the look of the work.

FLOORWORK   12 minutes

Legs

(1) Can you run and jump up high to show me different body shapes in the air?

(2) A long, stretched shape like a pencil looks very lively.

(3) A big star shape with arms and legs stretched wide is a very neat, strong shape to try.

(4) What other shapes are there? (Look out for and comment on twists and tucks with bent knees.)

Body

(1) Can you stand, balanced tall on tiptoes? It sometimes helps if you put one foot in front of the other. Stretch your arms out in front of you or to one side to help your balance.

(2) Slowly, can you lift one foot off the floor a little way and show me a new balance on just one foot? What strong body shape are you using to hold you nice and still?

(3) Now, can you lower down to sitting and roll back on to your shoulders to balance in a small, curled up shape?

(4) Now roll forwards again, right up to standing tall and stretched on tiptoes. Let's start all over again.

Arms

(1) As you travel slowly, using hands and feet, can you show me a long shape, a wide shape or a small, curled shape?

(2) Can you be very clever and go from a curled to a new shape as you travel carefully from space to space?

(3) Travelling with straight arms and legs is very difficult but strong. Can anyone show me travelling where your body parts are strong and straight?

APPARATUS WORK   16 minutes

(1) Run round the room without touching any apparatus. I hope that you are lifting your heels and your knees to make your running quiet and look good.

(2) When I call 'Stop!', show me a clear body shape on the nearest piece of apparatus. Make your body long, wide, curled, twisted or arched like a bridge. 'Stop!' (Repeat.)

(3) Now you can go on to all the apparatus. Try to find places where you can show me different body shapes. (For example, stretched hanging on a rope; standing wide on the climbing frame; curled up on a mat; lying stretched on a bench; arched across a box top.)

(4) Remember some of the ways you travelled on hands and feet on the floor. Can you do some of these actions, slowly and carefully, using the apparatus?

(5) Finally, you are going to travel on the apparatus and hold a balance somewhere. Then do a nicely, stretched jump up and off, followed by a beautiful, squashy landing.

FINAL FLOOR ACTIVITY   2 minutes

After a short run, show me a jump upwards with arms and legs stretched long or wide like a pencil or a star.

LESSON NOTES • 4 LESSONS DEVELOPMENT

FLOORWORK

Legs

(1) 'Can you...?' or 'Show me...' are expressions repeatedly used to give the pupils a new challenge.

(2) A teacher demonstration can be done in a standing position or, better still, moving, to show a very short run-up of two or three steps only.

(3) The star is difficult because they have to jump high enough to give time for the feet to come together before landing.

(4) If no suggestions are forthcoming, let the class all stand and feel a twist of one body part against another; or a tuck which can be practised in the crouch position with knees bent; or a bridge shape bent forwards, sideways or high backwards.

Body

(1) All follow the teacher into the tiptoes balance and hold it. 'Wobbling' is lessened by stretching arms to front or sides.

(2) Lift one foot a very small way if the balance is difficult. To help, the whole body can counterbalance by leaning slightly the other way.

(3) The slow lower to sitting down; the roll back on to shoulders; and the curled balance on shoulders should not be a problem if the back is kept rounded for the roll, with chin on chest.

(4) One long down-and-up swing from shoulders to standing again, pretending someone is pulling your arms to help.

Arms

(1) Much of the travelling will be crawling to start with. This can be developed by crawling on hands only, then on feet only, which means going from curled to stretched. Hands and feet can be close together, giving a long, narrow shape, or spread wide apart.

(2) The transfer from curled to stretched can be performed with front, back or side towards the floor, travelling on hands only, then on feet only.

(3) Travelling on straight arms and legs can be a normal crawling action or one where hands only travel first, then feet only. The body moves from a long, low position to a high hips position and works very strongly.

APPARATUS WORK

(1) 'Good running' is not common and continually needs to be asked for, explained and demonstrated.

(2) If the running has been well spaced out, the balances on the apparatus should be equally well spaced out and unimpeded. Good examples of wobble-free, firm, hard-working balances should be commented on, praised and demonstrated.

(3) Pupils go from apparatus to apparatus, holding a still position with an obvious shape as the challenge. They can be on, under, along, across, angled against the apparatus.

(4) To increase the class (and teacher's) repertoire, half the class at a time can demonstrate to the others a range of actions using hands and feet for travelling on apparatus.

(5) Travelling on floor on feet, and on hands and feet; travelling on all apparatus using hands and feet; held balances on apparatus; and the jump up and from apparatus, provide an exciting variety.

FINAL FLOOR ACTIVITY

All running together to one end of the room, jump up and stretch; all back to opposite end, jump high in a star.

LESSON PLAN • 30 MINUTES

Emphasis on: (a) an awareness of space, and of where you and others are going as you share the floor and the apparatus; (b) a caring attitude towards yourself and others as you move vigorously but safely on floor and apparatus; (c) working and practising hard to improve and enjoy the linking together of a series of actions.

FLOORWORK   12 minutes

Legs

(1) Can you keep travelling round the room on your feet, sometimes forwards and sometimes sideways?

(2) What actions do you think are good for going forwards? (Walking, running, skipping, hopping, for example.)

(3) What actions help you to travel sideways the best? Walking with small steps or lively skipping; feet together bouncing; galloping, for example.)

Body

(1) Show me a favourite, still balance, reaching high with both arms. No wobbling!

(2) Can you now reach out to the space in front or to one side of you, still balancing without wobbling?

(3) Can you choose a different part of your body now to balance on, reaching out to a low position to steady you? (The above sequence could include going from standing tall to leaning forwards on one foot, to crouching on hands and knees. Accompany each action with a reaching out to a different point in the surrounding space.)

Arms

(1) With all your weight on your hands, can you lift your feet up from the floor and put them down in a new place?

(2) Keep your arms straight for a strong position, and make your fingers point forwards.

(3) You can lift your feet from side to side over the lines on floor. You can jump them in between or outside your hands, perhaps twisting as you go.

APPARATUS WORK   16 minutes

(1) Can you travel up to, along and from a piece of apparatus, and show me a change of direction somewhere?

(2) Remember that your travelling is on both floor and apparatus. What neat ways are you using to travel on feet, or on hands and feet?

(3) A change of direction means that the side of your body or your back starts to lead the action, rather than the front of your body, as when you are going forwards.

(4) Be very careful if you go backwards. Look to see that you have plenty of space before stepping or jumping backwards.

(5) Show me travelling where you are low or near to the floor or apparatus. (Pulling along a bench; sliding down a plank; rolling on a mat; climbing, near to the frame; crawling under a plank, for example.)

(6) Use your feet only to travel up to and on to each piece of apparatus. Now show me a still, beautifully stretched balance high above the apparatus. Then jump down with a nice, squashy landing, and travel to the next piece of apparatus.

FINAL FLOOR ACTIVITY   2 minutes

Can you run and jump to land facing a new direction?

LESSON NOTES • 4 LESSONS DEVELOPMENT

FLOORWORK

Legs

(1) As the teacher says the words 'forwards' and 'sideways', he or she can show the meanings by moving forwards, then sideways.

(2) An emphasis on 'forwards' for a minute or two, giving examples if the class is not very forthcoming.

(3) A similar emphasis, but on 'sideways' this time. Explain that the side of your body leads when you are travelling sideways.

Body

(1) 'Balance' means that your body is on some unusual body part or apparatus surface and feels unsteady. We have to work hard not to wobble about. The reaching out here is to a *high* level.

(2) The reaching out in the second balance is to a *medium* level.

(3) The reaching out here is to a *low* level. These three levels are in our own surrounding air space. Levels, like directions and our own and general space, are elements of space which we use to give greater interest, variety and contrast to our gymnastic activities.

Arms

(1) The pupils are being given practice in 'feeling' where their feet are on the floor space that surrounds them. Strong arm and shoulder exercise accompanies this activity.

(2) This strong exercise is done most efficiently by keeping both arms straight, with fingers pointing forward as normal. Arms that bend are in a weak position. Fingers and hands pointing outwards do not work efficiently or safely.

(3) Suggestions from the teacher are necessary to develop this unusual activity of lifting feet from the floor and placing them down 'in a new place'. This activity will take place often on apparatus, and good, safe ideas and ways to perform on the floor will prove helpful later, on apparatus.

APPARATUS WORK

(1) The change of direction can be anywhere. Teacher commentary on the ideas seen and the places used for direction changes will add to the class repertoire. They can change direction after a rope swing; coming from a bench or low barbox; as they walk along a plank; as they travel on the climbing frame; as they travel on the floor between pieces of apparatus; after landing from a jump.

(2) Teacher commentary now can enthuse about the many travelling actions being practised and seen. Neat climbing, swinging, rolling, swinging, running and jumping, circling, skipping, bouncing, etc.

(3) Give them a reminder that they have to plan a direction change within their travelling up to, on, along and from the apparatus.

(4) It is helpful to stop the whole class and ask them to stand on a low piece of apparatus or a mat. 'Very carefully now, look behind you. If there is no-one in the way, step or jump off backwards to land softly and nicely balanced. Ready? Go!'

(5) Low level travelling means being near to the floor and apparatus, gripping strongly to pull, circle, swing, climb, slide, roll in close proximity to floor and apparatus.

(6) A high level stretch in contrast to the previous activity will take them well away from the apparatus.

FINAL FLOOR ACTIVITY

Facing a new direction is often necessary anyway when your run and jump take you near to a wall.

Reception Year • January • Lesson 5

LESSON PLAN • 30 MINUTES

Emphasis on: (a) travelling and experiencing the many ways that our feet, feet and hands, and large body surfaces can support and carry us; (b) an awareness of the many actions and uses of body parts that are possible as you travel.

FLOORWORK   12 minutes

Legs

(1) Can you walk, then run, jump and start your running again, without stopping?

(2) Because you are travelling without stopping, plan to make your walk and run short enough to give you plenty of room to do your lively jump and its landing, followed straight away by your next set of walking. No stopping!

(3) Travel along straight lines, never following anyone. Always look for good spaces in every part of the room.

Body

(1) Can you travel by going from a stretched to a curled body, using different parts of your body to support you?

(2) Can you lie on your back, stretched out; then curl up tight, holding your hands together under your knees; roll gently over on to one side; then stretch out long again?

(3) From standing tall and stretched up high, can you lower slowly down on to your seat to a curled sitting position? If you are very clever, you might rock back, still curled up small, then stretch up while balancing on your shoulders.

Arms

(1) Start in a curled, crouched position on hands and feet. Can you move your hands only until your body is long and stretched, then walk or jump your feet forwards, again to your curled, starting position?

(2) Do this very slowly so that your body is working hard. You can do it with feet and hands close together or wide apart. Which way feels harder?

(3) Can anyone show me another, slow way to travel using feet and hands? Demonstrate a selection of 'other ways' to help us remember.

APPARATUS WORK   16 minutes

(1) Travel without stopping to all parts of the room and do not touch any apparatus yet. Can you do your floorwork; walking, running and jumping without stopping? (For example, walking across, under, through; running on floor, across mats, astride benches; jumping over mats, benches, low planks.)

(2) Use your feet only now to bring you on to, take you along and bring you off the apparatus. Plan to show me a good variety of actions. (For example, step, jump or bounce on; walk, skip, bounce, run, hop, balance along; step, jump or swing up and off.)

(3) Now travel slowly, using hands and feet, up to, on, along and from each piece of apparatus in turn. Travel slowly so that I can easily see your strong, neat actions.

(4) On floor and apparatus, can you travel by changing from a long, stretched shape to a round, curled shape? Your curled shape can sometimes take you into a roll to travel to your next stretch.

(5) You can stretch and curl your way across the climbing frame; on and under planks, poles and benches; and rolling across mats.

FINAL FLOOR ACTIVITY   2 minutes

Show me a way to travel silently using your feet.

14

LESSON NOTES • 4 LESSONS DEVELOPMENT

FLOORWORK

Legs

(1) Three or four walking steps following by four or five running steps provide a nice, reasonably short rhythm before the 'Jump and start walking again'.

(2) The lively jump will be done with full swing up of the arms. This arm action, plus a 'give' of the knees and ankles on landing, helps to balance and control you as you land.

(3) With young primary school pupils we continually have to ask them not to circulate in a curving, anti-clockwise direction. By moving in a straight line, they will seldom be following anyone, and the direction changes needed as they come to the outside take them to all parts of the room space.

Body

(1) To help them to get the idea and get started, we can show them a crouch position, on feet only, curled down near the floor. Then we can take them into a big stretch up and step forwards, one foot after the other, to standing tall.

(2) Alternating whole body stretches and curls is most easily done while lying down with front, back or side towards the floor.

(3) This little sequence takes them from a high to a lower level as well as from a stretch to a curl, and includes lowering and rolling as linking movements.

Arms

(1) Emphasise the straight arms for a safe, strong position, particularly if there is a moment when the hands take all the weight as the feet are jumped forwards.

(2) If the legs as well as the arms are kept straight, a high, arched dome shape alternates with the long, low, straight shape.

(3) They can travel with back towards floor; with feet or one side leading rather than head; with bunny jumps or cartwheels.

APPARATUS WORK

(1) Planning to walk, then run, then jump somewhere and carry on walking without stopping gives them a good challenge.

(2) Thoughtful travelling on feet only calls for well controlled steps, jumps and bounces, and good, safe, sensible landing actions.

(3) A wide variety of ways to grip, hold and support yourself on, around, across and under the apparatus are practised here.

(4) 'Hands only first. Feet only next.' Crouch to stretch to crouch is the simplest way to alternate between these two shapes. This is done easily on mats, benches, boxes, planks and on one side of the climbing frame.

(5) Stand, roll, stand; lie straight, curl, lie straight; bring hands and feet close together, then take them apart on floor, on top of and under surfaces; or swing on a rope with a curled body and land with a straight body. These are all ways to answer this task.

FINAL FLOOR ACTIVITY

The teacher, using a very quiet voice, can say 'While you are travelling, using your feet silently, I will keep my eyes closed. I don't want to hear a sound. Can you make me think that no-one is moving in the hall?'

15

Reception Year • February • Lesson 6

LESSON PLAN • 30 MINUTES

Emphasis on: (a) planning and performing basic actions, including jumping and landing, rolling and taking weight on hands; (b) showing concern for self and others by good behaviour and sensible sharing of space.

FLOORWORK   12 minutes

Legs

(1) Can you do some little bouncing jumps in your own space, then run to a space near you and do another jump?

(2) The bouncing jumps will be quiet if you push off with your toes, and let your knees and ankles bend softly on landing.

(3) Can you land from your running jump and be still, without any wobbling about? Arms that stretch out in front can help you to land and balance nicely.

Body

(1) Can you sit down with your back all rounded and your head down on your knees? Now try to rock backwards and forwards, with your body rolling like a ball, all the way from your seat to your shoulders. Backwards and forwards; roll backwards and forwards.

(2) Now can you lie flat on your back with your hands clasped together under your knees, making you round and small? Try a little rock from side to side now.

(3) Can you join up for me a little rock backwards and forwards, then side to side? Keep your back curled and head forwards on knees, just like a rolling ball.

Arms

(1) Stand and hold your hands in front towards me. Keep the arms straight. Bend down and put your hands on the floor. Can you push on your hands, and jump over your feet up off the floor?

(2) We can call this 'bunny jumping'. Keep your head looking forwards and your arms strong and straight.

(3) Keep your legs bent, and push feet hard against floor.

(4) Keep your hands pointing forwards and your fingers spread.

APPARATUS WORK   16 minutes

(1) At all the low pieces of apparatus, let me see you using your feet only to bring you on to the apparatus. (For example, step, jump, bounce or run on to benches, barbox top, barbox bottom, planks or mats.)

(2) Jump down from your low apparatus on to the mat, and show me a beautifully soft, squashy landing, which can take you right down slowly on to your back. Then you can do a little roll sideways right over on to your front. Jump up, and off you go again!

(3) Once again, hold your arms out towards me, showing me straight arms. Walk round, putting both hands on each piece of apparatus and jump your feet off the floor. Keep your head looking forwards, not back under your arms.

(4) As you come towards each piece of apparatus, can you do a little upwards jump on your spot, then walk, jog or run up to the apparatus and carefully take the weight on your hands?

(5) Walk round now, visiting each of the mats, and have a little go at your rocking and rolling movements that we practised in the floorwork. Sit down, see that you have room and then practise forwards and backwards or side to side.

FINAL FLOOR ACTIVITY   2 minutes

Can you do sets of four jumps, turning to face a different side of the hall each time? Jump, 2, 3, 4 and turn; jump, 2, 3, 4 and turn.

16

FLOORWORK

Legs

(1) The main features of jumping or bouncing on the spot are a good stretch in the ankle joint and a push off from the balls of the feet. One or two good demonstrators will give the class a picture of what is wanted.

(2) The knees, ankles and hips all 'give' like springs on landing. This 'giving', soft cushioning, recoiled landing is particularly important in landing safely from a height.

(3) The jump after the run will be a forwards one, contrasting with the starting jump upwards. To help balance a forwards jump, hold straight arms out in front at shoulder height.

Body

(1) If class mirror the teacher who sits down at front with knees bent, back rounded, chin down on chest, they will be in a good position straight away.

(2) A swing to the side by the knees takes you sideways. Demonstrate with a good example the importance of the well rounded back for easy rocking.

(3) 'Backwards and forwards; one side, the other side; to shoulders, to seat; to left and to right.'

Arms

(1) All stand facing teacher, holding both arms straight out in front to show the straight arm position, fingers pointing forwards. This is the basis for a strong, safe, ungiving arm position when all the body weight is on the hands only.

(2) If the head looks backwards under the arms instead of forwards, everything will be upside down and the pupils will be disorientated. 'Look forwards to see everything normally.'

(3) Bent legs are short levers which can be lifted quickly.

(4) We need to remind them to place both hands strongly facing forwards, not out to the sides as often happens.

APPARATUS WORK

(1) We focused on the importance of hands in the previous activity on the floor. Now we are focusing on the feet and the many varied, neat actions that they can perform at apparatus.

(2) A jump down which flows slowly and carefully into a squashy landing on the mat is an enjoyable sequence – firm, straight, vigorous jump high from apparatus contrasting with a soft, easy, curled roll down at low level.

(3) With straight arms, they now visit each piece of apparatus and perform a little bunny jump, momentarily taking all the weight on the hands only. 'Straight arms and bent legs, and keep looking forwards.'

(4) A little jump on the spot before travelling, as practised at the start of the floorwork, gives an added momentum to the bunny jumps on the apparatus, making them easier.

(5) The ten or so mats in a well provided hall provide ample opportunities for practising the favourite rolling action in comfort. Moving round until you see a quiet space on a mat is also an exercise in 'showing concern for self and others.'

FINAL FLOOR ACTIVITY

All can face the front, then the side being pointed to by the teacher, then the back, then the other side, then back to the front again, enjoying working together in unison.

LESSON PLAN • 30 MINUTES

Emphasis on: (a) partner work to provide new experiences and develop desirable social relationships; (b) being interested in and able to observe simple actions, and to copy, describe and learn from pleasing features.

FLOORWORK   11 minutes

Legs

(1) From a still starting position, one partner performs a short travel, a jump and landing, and a still, balanced finish. The other partner observes and copies.

(2) Can you improve your sequence by showing a good body shape at the beginning, in your jump, and at the end?

(3) Watching partner, did you see how many feet your partner jumped from? Was it one or both?

(4) Are you landing with feet together or apart, or even with one foot after the other?

Body and Arms

(1) One partner makes a shape like a bridge, supported on hands and feet. The other partner travels underneath, over, across, through, in and out of this bridge shape, without touching the still partner.

(2) Change places and repeat the activity. The new bridge-making partner can be on hands and feet, or some other parts for support. Can the travelling partner go under, across, through or in and out of this new bridge without touching it?

(3) Keep on practising in your own time, making a still, strong bridge, then travelling, one after the other.

(4) If you are taking a lot of weight on your hands when making a bridge or travelling under or over, remember to keep your arms straight for a safe, strong support.

APPARATUS WORK   16 minutes

(1) Follow your leader up to and on to each piece of apparatus, and show a beautifully clear body shape in a still, balanced position. One after the other, leave your apparatus, travel to the next piece and show me another still balance with a clear body shape.

(2) As you travel on the floor between apparatus, are you trying to copy your partner's travelling actions? If I asked you to show me, would you both be doing the same actions?

(3) The other partner will lead now. Can you show me some travelling, both on floor and apparatus, where you use your arms strongly? (This can include hands only and a bunny jump on apparatus or floor.)

(4) It helps if the leader goes first, travels a little distance and then waits for the partner (who has stood still, watching the leader very carefully) to follow.

FINAL FLOOR ACTIVITY   3 minutes

Take turns at follow the leader and show your following partner your favourite way or ways to travel neatly and quietly using your feet, e.g. walking, running, jumping, skipping, hopping, bouncing, slipping sideways, hopscotch.

LESSON NOTES • 4 LESSONS DEVELOPMENT

FLOORWORK

Legs

(1) It helps if a couple chooses and stays in a small area of the room, free from the distraction of other couples, and works backwards and forwards on their own private 'stage'. The alternative is usually a circle of pairs getting in each others' way as they push up against the couple in front.

(2) A good body shape means you are working hard (no lazy sagging); improving the appearance of the performance; and showing good body control, one of several reasons why we do physical education.

(3) The usual one-footed take-off is best for a long jump. The less common two-footed take-off is best for an upward, high jump.

(4) Landing with one foot after the other helps to slow you down gradually for a more controlled finish. However, landing on two feet is the usual method practised.

Body and Arms

(1) If the pupils are asked 'Can anyone point out a bridge-like shape in the room?', someone will point to a trestle, the outline of the barbox, or the side walls and ceiling of the room. This gives them a picture of the arched shapes we are looking for.

(2) The front, back or one side of the body can be facing the floor. The bridge can be on hands and knees; hands and feet; under knees while seated; under knees while lying; under front, back or side of body while the bridge-maker is standing with body arched.

(3) Pointing out examples of different level bridges – high on feet only; medium on hands and feet only; low lying on back or front with a shallow bridge – extends the class repertoire and the ways of negotiating that can be experimented with.

(4) With back or front to the floor, and on hands and feet only, it is important to keep the arms firm and straight. It is also good exercise for parts of your body seldom exercised strongly.

APPARATUS WORK

(1) If they follow the leader at a distance of 2–3 metres, they will be able to observe and copy the actions; the exact use of the body parts concerned; and the body shapes used in the travelling. For the 'clear body shape in a still balance' on apparatus, the leader will need to wait for the follower to join him or her on the apparatus and hold still for two or three seconds as a pair.

(2) A demonstration by a good leading and following couple, moving almost as one, is recommended. Half of the class at a time can be asked to show their still balances to identify the many supporting body parts possible. The majority will be on feet only. We want balances on seat; shoulders; one hand and one foot; tummy across plank or bench; one foot only, etc.

(3) Using your arms strongly when travelling, make full use now of all the apparatus, being sensible to ensure that there is enough room for you and your partner.

(4) 'Leader, travel a short distance, then stop and wait for your partner to copy you and catch up.' This will break the activity down into: (a) the travel on the floor; (b) the mount and travel along the apparatus; and (c) the dismount and leaving the apparatus. A neat, tall, still position at start and finish each time enhances the impression and the appearance enormously.

FINAL FLOOR ACTIVITY

Each can lead two or three times, giving time for seeing, copying and mirroring exactly.

Reception Year • April • Lesson 8

LESSON PLAN • 30 MINUTES

Emphasis on: (a) planning and practising to link two or three actions together; (b) demonstrating greater confidence through neat, controlled work.

FLOORWORK   12 minutes

Legs
(1) Can you do an upwards jump where you are, then show me a very short run and another high jump?
(2) In each jump, can you stretch your whole body beautifully?
(3) When you land, can you let your knees and ankles 'give' softly and quietly?

Body
(1) Show me a favourite, still body shape. (Stretched, arched, wide, curled, twisted or bridge-like.)
(2) Can you move on to a different part of your body and show me a new body shape?
(3) Try to make up a little sequence of three joined-up and different body shapes that you can remember and repeat.

Arms
(1) Bend your knees, crouch down and put your hands flat on the floor just in front of you. Your weight is now supported on your hands and feet.
(2) Can you show me two or three ways to lift your feet off the floor and then put them down quietly in a different place?
(3) You can lift them and put them down on the same spot; or twist to one side; or lift the feet to go forwards, outside or between your hands.

APPARATUS WORK   16 minutes

(1) Stand tall on tiptoes, showing me a beautifully still, stretched body shape. Now travel up to and on to a piece of apparatus and show me a still, firm body shape. Leave your first piece of apparatus, travel and stop in a new floor space, once again showing me your beautifully stretched body. (Repeat up to and on to the next piece of apparatus.)
(2) From your own floor space, can you make your hands important as you travel up to, on to, along and from each piece of apparatus in turn? Finish back in your own space on the floor.

(3) Keep both arms straight and strong as you put hands only on the apparatus. Lift bent legs off the floor to take all the weight on your hands. You can put your feet down on the same spot or a new one (e.g. to cross a bench).
(4) Stay at the piece of apparatus where you are now. Can you be very clever and join together for me: (a) a still, stretched, balanced starting position; (b) your way of travelling up to and on to the apparatus, using feet only or both feet and hands; (c) a still position on the apparatus with a clear body shape; (d) a neat, still finishing position, away from the apparatus, on the floor?

FINAL FLOOR ACTIVITY   2 minutes

Can you run and jump high, then run and jump long?

20

FLOORWORK

Legs
(1) A very short run of two or three strides only will take them to a nearby space for the second jump. They should almost feel and hear their rhythm 'Jump; run, run, run and jump.'
(2) The stretch while in the air should extend from the top of the head right down to the pointed toes. This is neat, looks good and 'correct', and makes the work more demanding and physical.
(3) The squashy landing makes this, and landings from a greater height, quiet and safe.

Body
(1) For a quick start, all can do a standing, tall, stretched body shape, mirroring the teacher. Emphasise the firm feeling, with no lazily sagging parts, and the complete stillness in position.
(2) If help is needed to move them on to their next and different position and shape, the teacher can offer 'Your seat; your knees; your shoulders; on to one foot only; your back, front or side; one hand and one foot.'
(3) If a demonstration is arranged, the class can be asked to look out for 'Which body parts were supported? What shapes did you see? What movements were used to link them together?'

Arms
(1) Flat hands point forwards, about shoulder width apart, and the arms are kept straight. These important points for a safe, strong support can be taught as a whole class activity before they start.
(2) The perfect position for a bunny jump has shoulders above hips above hands. Bent legs lift higher more easily than straighter ones.
(3) One landing on the same spot; one that twists to one side or over a line; one where you reach forwards on to hands (in a new floor space) and pull legs up to a new place. These provide a good mixture.

APPARATUS WORK

(1) We are aiming to develop a *pattern* which will apply in nearly all apparatus work henceforth, namely: (a) a still, ready, starting position in own floor space; (b) a travel up to and on to the apparatus; (c) an activity that they have been challenged to do while on the apparatus; (d) a coming away from the apparatus to finish; (e) still and tall, in a floor space.
(2) On ropes, climbing frames, trestles, planks and poles, benches and barboxes, hand activity is important. The class are being made aware of the many ways that we grip, support, pull, hang, climb, circle or twist across the varied pieces of apparatus.
(3) 'Hands on, feet off; move to new place.' Head looks forwards, not back under arms, so that we see things the right way up, not upside down. Bent legs are short levers which make the lift up off the floor easier.
(4) Ask them to keep their little sequences 'little' as they plan to include the five elements requested. Proud, confident, still starting and finishing positions can be praised and shown.

FINAL FLOOR ACTIVITY

A short run to make the jumps the main part.

LESSON PLAN • 30 MINUTES

Emphasis on: (a) experiencing the use of different degrees of speed and force to contribute variety and contrast to performances; (b) enthusiastic participation in physical activity and believing that these lessons are fun, good for you and exciting.

FLOORWORK   12 minutes

Legs

(1) Can you walk forwards very slowly on tiptoes and, when you see an empty space near you, run, speeding up, and show me an explosive high jump?

(2) Be very still each time before you start. Still; then slow walk; then speed up and explode!

(3) Can you feel nice and loose as you walk, and feel strong as you run and jump?

Body

(1) Can you show me a balance with part of your body firm and stretched? (For example on tiptoes with arms stretched; on one foot with non-supporting leg stretched; seated with arms and legs stretched; on shoulders with both legs stretched.)

(2) Can you relax and gently move on to another part or parts to balance strongly again,

stretching part of your body? (Linking movements are rolls, lowers, twists.)

(3) Keep going and try to do two or three, all nicely linked.

(4) Can you 'feel' the difference between the strong stretch and the easy, relaxed way you change between them?

Arms

(1) Pretend you are a kicking horse as you take all the weight on both hands and kick your feet backwards and forwards in the air. Make the kicks strong and fast, like the rear legs of a horse.

(2) Horses, can you come back down to the floor with very gentle and quiet feet?

(3) Keep your arms long and straight for a strong position, and look forwards with your head, not back under the arms which makes everything appear upside down.

APPARATUS WORK   16 minutes

(1) Show me a mixture of slow, relaxed travelling away from apparatus (e.g. walking, easy jogging, skipping) with hardly a sound from anyone. Remember to visit all parts of the room; the sides, ends, corners and the middle.

(2) Show me a strong action as you work near the apparatus, still without touching it (e.g. run and jump over parts of mats; bounce along astride benches; swing into high jump across a low plank).

(3) Using all the apparatus now, can you get on to it using your hands strongly, and travel using

hands and feet?

(4) Start on the floor near the apparatus and show me a balance on tiptoes or on one foot only, with a part of your body stretched strongly. Relax and travel up to the apparatus to show me a new balance, not on feet only, with a part of your body stretched strongly.

(5) Can you show me a lively, vigorous jump from low apparatus, then a soft, squashy landing and an easy, relaxed roll sideways on your mat?

FINAL FLOOR ACTIVITY   2 minutes

ome soft, slow, quiet jumps on the spot, then run into a speeding up high jump.

FLOORWORK

Legs

(1) Emphasise that it is a very short run only into the explosive high jump. Some pupils will run all round the room with very few jumps being practised. They can be asked to 'Walk... now stop! Can you point to a good space very near you? Get ready to run two or three steps, speeding up into your high jump... Go!

(2) The interesting contrasts here are: stillness; slow motion; acceleration; stillness.

(3) The class can be asked 'Does your body feel different when you walk and when you speed up for your jump?', to describe changes in body tension.

Body

(1) Explain that 'balance' means being on some small or unusual part or parts of your body and not wobbling, although you feel unsteady.

(2) The parts being stretched are those parts not being used to support you.

(3) A simple trio could include: standing; lower to sitting; roll back to shoulder balance.

(4) The strong, hard working, unsagging stretch contrasts with the easy, giving, relaxed linking movements.

Arms

(1) Kicking while on the hands is easier than trying to hold a handstand balance with feet together. The rapid leg movements seem to help the balancing.

(2) Legs bend from the straight kicking to come down gently to the floor.

(3) Straight arms and hands at shoulder width pointing forwards are the main teaching points.

APPARATUS WORK

(1) The planning requested here is for easy, soft, slow action and a good use of all the space for the sake of self and others.

(2) Greater effort is now called for to negotiate apparatus, still without touching it.

(3) Strong hand positions include the thumbs under grip on bars; hands together when swinging on a rope; gripping at sides of bench, planks and low barbox; and the straight arms

on flat surfaces as you vault or bunny jump across.

(4) A pattern of: a firm, still, stretched balance; a relaxed, easy travel; a firm, still, stretched balance.

(5) The contrast between the strong, stretched, explosive leap up and off to a high level, and the gentle, relaxed, rounded roll at low level, makes for an attractive and varied performance.

FINAL FLOOR ACTIVITY

Almost slow motion, soft jumping on the spot, needs a full bend and stretch in the ankle and knee joints, and a good, high action. In the speeding up run, they can pretend to be springing up and on to a bench.

Reception Year • June • Lesson 10

LESSON PLAN • 30 MINUTES

Emphasis on: (a) partner work because it is good fun and interesting, and lets you do new activities you could not do on your own; (b) watching another and answering questions on what was seen and liked.

FLOORWORK   12 minutes

Legs
(1) Follow your leader who will show you two or three different actions to copy, using legs only.
(2) Keep about two steps behind your leader so that you can see what his or her feet are doing.
(3) Leader, if it is crowded, you can do an action on the spot.

Body
(1) The new leader will demonstrate a nice, clear body shape for the partner to copy. You can be stretched long; curled like a ball; wide like a star; arched like a bridge; or twisted.
(2) The same leader now changes slowly to a new, clear body shape, and might need to do it on a new part of the body. Partner watches and copies. (For example a smooth change from a high stretch, standing, down to a curled crouch, still on both feet.)
(3) Leader, can you show your partner and me a third and last new body shape, please? (For example a smooth change from crouch to a bridge-like shape, standing, with upper body arched forwards, arms pointing down to floor.)

Arms
(1) Travel side by side, moving hands only, then feet only. Try to move in unison.
(2) Two of you need a lot of room. Move towards the best space you can see.
(3) Are you moving with hands and feet close together or wide apart? Remember to keep your arms straight for a strong support.

APPARATUS WORK   16 minutes

(1) Follow your leader in and out of all the apparatus, without touching any yet. Can you travel on straight lines, not following anyone else? I would like to see two or three travelling actions.
(2) Now the other partner will lead as you travel up to each piece of apparatus, on to or across it for a very short time, then away from it. (No long travels or lingering on apparatus.)
(3) Can you start at opposite sides or ends of a piece of apparatus and travel to cross to your partner's side? (Both may move at same time, space permitting, on climbing frames or mats, across barbox or plank. On narrow apparatus, one may need to cross first before second moves.)
(4) As you cross the apparatus this time, can you stop for a moment to show your partner and me a whole body shape that you like to make somewhere on the apparatus?

FINAL FLOOR ACTIVITY   2 minutes

Stand facing each other. Now jump up and down quietly, with a good stretch in your ankles. Can you be very clever and bounce together at the same time?

24

FLOORWORK

Legs

(1) Teacher commentary on actions observed will help to inspire a more varied response. 'I see good stepping, running, hopping, bouncing, jumping, hopscotch, skipping and slipping.' (A quick demonstration of neat, well-controlled, varied activities will be productive.)

(2) When observing actions we look out for: the action itself; the way that body parts are working; any interesting shapes that are being used. (For example, skipping, with high knees and arms well lifted, and bent legs and straight arms.)

(3) 'On the spot, then moving' is always an interesting and varied use of floor space and worth encouraging.

Body

(1) Early in the lesson's development it is a good idea to suggest doing this while on one or both feet. All the shapes possible can be shown while on the feet, and it gets everything moving quickly.

(2) A very slow change from shape to shape will enable the following partner to do it at the same time, saving waiting and watching time, and leading to more action.

(3) 'Good things happen in threes.' A sequence with three parts is short enough to be remembered, but long enough to be varied and interesting.

Arms

(1) Very slow travel on hands and then feet means that the body is working hard to support itself, and that both partners can work in unison, which is particularly pleasurable.

(2) When travelling on hands and feet, young pupils often tend to move in towards the centre of the room. Encourage travelling out to the extremities where there is more space.

(3) Hands and feet close together makes a high arch. When hands and feet are apart after the hands alone have gone forwards, the low arch position created is difficult to hold.

APPARATUS WORK

(1) Demonstrate with two or three couples, whose spacing and choice of neat and varied actions is admirable.

(2) A 'quick on to and off the apparatus' suggests jumps over; bunny jumps across; twists across; a short swing on a rope; or a roll across a mat.

(3) From facing each other on opposite sides travel a short way up to, on to, along, around or across the apparatus; then a short distance to partner's starting place on the floor.

(4) Let them repeat it two or three times where they are, then demonstrations by half of the class at a time. This shows them good ideas to use when they change round to work at a new piece of apparatus.

FINAL FLOOR ACTIVITY

Slow, quiet jumps need a good, high lift from a strong stretch of the ankles, followed by a soft 'give' in knees, ankles and hips on landing.

Reception Year • July • Lesson 11

LESSON PLAN • 30 MINUTES

Emphasis on: (a) planning and performing short, simple sequences of two or three movements linked together to produce a pleasing performance; (b) reflecting that they have looked forward to and enjoyed taking part in vigorous action in these lessons during the past year.

FLOORWORK   12 minutes

Legs
(1) Show me two ways to walk, run, jump and land, including a still start and finish each time.
(2) What body shape are you holding at start and finish, and in your jump? Think about it and make it clear.
(3) What actions are you using as you take off and land?
Body
(1) Change from being curled up small to a different body shape. Then change back again to being tightly curled.
(2) From what curled, starting position can you easily change to your different shape? (For example, crouched on both feet; lying on side;

lying on back; kneeling; tightly curled on both shoulders.)
(3) A sequence of three parts, curled and not curled, neatly and slowly joined together, would be very interesting.
Arms
(1) Can you show me two or three ways to take all the weight on to your hands? (For example, 'kicking horses'; bunny jumps; cartwheels; handstands.)
(2) Remember to keep both arms straight for a safe, strong position.
(3) Keep your hands and your head looking forwards.

APPARATUS WORK   16 minutes

(1) Travel all round the room, changing smoothly from one way of moving to a new one. Do not touch any apparatus yet, but you may go over, across, under, along or in and out.
(2) Start off in a still, nicely balanced position on the floor. Travel up to and on to a piece of apparatus, and show me a neat, still, balanced position. Then move away from the apparatus to a new starting position on the floor, and begin again at the next piece of apparatus.
(3) Travel on apparatus and floor, showing your shapes clearly. (For example, curled up rolls;

stretched pulls on plank and bench; tucked up bunny jumps over bench or low barbox; star or stretched jumps up and from all apparatus.)
(4) Can you travel all over the room, showing me your favourite ways to travel up to, on, along and from apparatus?
(5) On the apparatus I would like to see travelling across, around, under, along, up and down – lots of variety, using the many different body actions you have practised, learned and enjoyed, I hope, this year.

FINAL FLOOR ACTIVITY   2 minutes

Stand tall and still. Lower slowly to sitting. Rock backwards with head on chest and back nicely rounded. Clasp hands under knees. Roll to one side, right over on to your front. Jump up and repeat.

LESSON NOTES • 4 LESSONS DEVELOPMENT

FLOORWORK

Legs

(1) Like sentries, they can go forwards and backwards in their own space corridor of 3–4 metres, not being disturbed or disturbing others.

(2) Shape is often dictated by what the arms are doing – at sides, stretched up, out to sides or forwards. The jump shape will be a long stretch, a wide star, a curled tuck, or a (difficult) jacknife.

(3) The 'take-off and landing' refer to the jump. This could be from one or both feet, landing with both feet together or apart, one foot in front of the other, or one landing after the other.

Body

(1) 'Everyone curl up tight and small. Keep your chin on your chest. Elbows in, round back.' Give this starting challenge, letting them choose their own bases to be curled on. If the response is poor, they can copy one of the class or the teacher.

(2) The varied starting positions can be identified and looked at as ideas for the continuing changes.

(3) Particularly attractive is a sequence where the stretching is to different levels. (For example, curled crouch on both feet to high stretched standing; back to same curl; lower to low stretch, lying on back; curl on side; up to kneeling, stretching arms to a medium level in space.)

Arms

(1) 'All weight on hands' means that feet have to leave the floor at some point. During the past year, on floor and on apparatus, they will have done this many times and seen many good examples.

(2) 'Correct' technique needs to be continually checked. Arms that bend are weak and will give way. A straight arm is a safe prop.

(3) If you look back under your arms, everything appears to be upside down. 'Head forwards' is even more important when taking weight on hands only, on apparatus.

APPARATUS WORK

(1) At this stage of the year, pupils should be able to demonstrate neat, well controlled, well spaced and varied travelling on floor. Adventurous negotiating of apparatus without touching it is also required here.

(2) Balanced start; travel; balanced finish, going from apparatus to apparatus challenges them to make quick decisions to cope with different situations.

(3) Be aware of making a shape at all times. If we make it a firm, whole body shape (not lazy or sagging), the work becomes more demanding and the performance greatly enhanced.

(4) All gymnasts have their favourite routines that they enjoy doing almost without thinking. The teacher has to look out for, praise and coach the actions being presented, so that the 'favourite' is also the best routine.

(5) Reception pupils often start school with little experience of the climbing, swinging, circling, jumping, hanging under, pulling and sliding that are typical in a lively gymnastic activities lesson. It is hoped that they are now less inhibited, more confident and more skilful at all these natural body movements.

FINAL FLOOR ACTIVITY

The sideways roll is a half turn from being on the back to being on the front. The impetus for the sideways roll comes from a swing of both bent knees to one side.

Year 1 • September • Lesson 1

LESSON PLAN • 30 MINUTES

Emphasis on: (a) the unselfish sharing of space with a concern for own and others' safety, and immediate responses to instructions; (b) neat, well planned use of feet and hands in travelling on floor and apparatus; (c) lifting, carrying, placing and using apparatus quietly, carefully and safely, in co-operation with others.

FLOORWORK   12 minutes

Legs
(1) Walk quietly in and out of one another, visiting every part of the room. Don't follow anyone.
(2) Now show me your best running, moving along straight lines, not curving around, all following one another. Go to the corners, ends and sides as well as the middle.
(3) Plan to show me some other way or ways you can travel, using your feet. (For example, skip, hop, bounce, gallop, slip, jump.)
Body
(1) Run a few steps into a space near you, jump up high, and then do a soft, squashy landing. Spring up, look for a new space, and off you go again.

(2) If you land with your feet a little bit apart, it is easier to balance still in your squashy, bent legs position.
(3) Stretch arms above head in the jump, and forwards or sideways to balance you on landing. See which helps you better.
Arms
(1) As you travel about slowly, using hands and feet only, can you make different parts of your body go first?
(2) Try leading with head, feet, or one side of your body.
(3) Can you plan some actions where only your hands travel, then only your feet?

APPARATUS WORK   16 minutes

(1) Travel to all parts of the room without touching any apparatus. Use your feet only, and show me how you can go in and out of, along, across or under the apparatus, touching mats only.
(2) Look for quiet places where you have lots of room. You can step or jump over benches, weave in and out of ropes, walk astride or along benches, jump across parts of the mats, or squeeze through spaces in the climbing frames.
(3) When I call 'Stop!', find a space on the nearest apparatus, and show me a fully stretched body. Now jump down quietly, and off you go again, travelling and listening for my

next signal.
(4) Using feet only, show me how you can travel up to, on to, along and from the apparatus. Remember, feet only, and show me lots of good travelling on the floor as well as on apparatus.
(5) Use your hands and feet to travel on the floor, up to, on to, along and down from the apparatus. Once again, you can use a jump and a squashy landing.
(6) Plan to visit many different pieces of apparatus. 'Feel' the different ways that your hands and feet can support you. (You can hang, swing, crawl, circle, climb, roll, slide.)

FINAL FLOOR ACTIVITY   2 minutes

Walk, run, jump, skip and bounce in and out of one another. Visit all parts of the room.

FLOORWORK

Legs

(1) Right from the start of the year we have to work against the almost habitual, anti-clockwise travelling of primary school pupils, all following one another as they curve round the outside.

(2) Challenge them to visit ends, sides, corners and centre, going there along a straight line and changing direction as soon as they find themselves following another.

(3) Teacher commentary on the varied actions helps to expand the class repertoire. Quick demonstrations provide pictures that are remembered, copied and tried.

Body

(1) The whole body is working strongly in the fully stretched position while in the air. From the upward stretch in both arms down to the stretched ankles, the whole body should feel firm.

(2) Feet can be slightly apart, side by side or one in front of the other. The squashy 'giving' landing contrasts with the firm spring upwards.

(3) Pupils experiment to see whether arms stretched forwards or sideways help them balance better in the landings.

Arms

(1) 'Different parts going first' would stop them all crawling forwards with bent arms and legs – the usual first response and often done far too quickly to have any physical benefits.

(2) Show good examples of actions with different parts leading, and emphasise 'Slow movements using the whole body strongly; straight arms for a safe, strong support; clear body shapes to add to the appearance of the performance.'

(3) From a crouch position, hands and feet close together, move hands only forwards until body is fully stretched; then feet travel, either walking forwards or with a jump in. Hands and feet can be close together or wide apart, which is harder.

APPARATUS WORK

(1) Occasionally, stop the travelling to check that all are moving, well spaced apart, never following another and in a variety of relationships to the apparatus.

(2) Teacher commentary on interesting activities to negotiate apparatus helps to inspire variety.

(3) 'Stop!' is an exercise in 'immediate responses to instructions', and must be answered straight away. Poor responses waste time as all wait for the casual responder to decide when to co-operate.

(4) Neat, quiet travelling on the floor between apparatus should be praised and demonstrated. Point out interesting actions and uses of feet and legs. On to and from the apparatus will be a short travel, mostly walking, jumping, tiptoeing or bouncing.

(5) This favourite part of the lesson, when all can go anywhere on the apparatus, is exciting, challenging and good fun. Hands and feet must both be used in travelling freely on all pieces. Look out for and comment on the varied activities going on to help the less inventive with new ideas.

(6) We want them to experience and understand how their bodies are working, and to feel relaxed and better after vigorous activity.

FINAL FLOOR ACTIVITY

Challenge them 'Can you join three of your favourite activities together?'

Year 1 • October • Lesson 2

LESSON PLAN • 30 MINUTES

Emphasis on: (a) wholehearted, vigorous activity to inspire enjoyment, achievement and a sense of well-being and calm; (b) variety in travelling on feet, and feet and hands, including climbing and swinging; (c) co-operating sensibly with others to lift, carry, place and use apparatus.

FLOORWORK   12 minutes

Legs

(1) Can you run a few steps and jump up high, with feet together and long straight legs?

(2) Now, can you run and jump up high, showing a wide body shape like a star, with arms and legs wide stretched?

(3) With a neat, tall start and finish position, can you now alternate these different jumps, using only a run of 3 metres each way?

Body

(1) Stand with feet slightly apart. Swing both arms forwards to a full stretch above head. With a long, slow, bouncy action, bend knees and swing arms down behind, forwards, behind, then swing arms forwards and up above head again, with a lifting up of the body.

(2) It's like a ski swing. Stretch up; bend down; bounce arms backwards, forwards, backwards; swing up tall again.

Arms

(1) Can you try to travel on hands and feet, keeping them wide apart? (For example, cartwheels; bouncing along on all fours; crawling with left side moving, then right side moving; wide hands only, then wide feet only.)

(2) Now, can you travel with hands and feet close together? For example, bunny jumps along; close hands, then close feet travel.

APPARATUS WORK   16 minutes

(1) Jog round the room without stopping, touching only the floor and the mats. Can you visit each piece of apparatus and go under, over, across, along, in and out of it, always without touching?

(2) When I call 'Stop!', can you show me a beautifully long or wide stretched, still body on the nearest piece of apparatus?

(3) Jump down quietly and continue travelling on the floor only until my next signal. Then show me your stretched or wide shape on a new body part and a new piece of apparatus.

(4) On the floor between apparatus, practise again your short run and jump with high and wide body shapes. On the apparatus, find out how many ways you can support yourself with good hands and feet actions.

(5) How are your hands and feet positioned when gripping a rope or a metal pole; when rolling across a mat; when bunny jumping up and over a bench or box top; when climbing the frame; when pulling along a bench; when circling round a bar?

FINAL FLOOR ACTIVITY   2 minutes

Run a few steps into a high jump, arms stretched high above head. Land with a good, squashy, knees bent action, arms above head. Now revise the slow ski swings; down behind, forwards, backwards and all the way up. Lower arms, and off again. Strong jumps and easy ski swings.

LESSON NOTES • 4 LESSONS DEVELOPMENT

FLOORWORK

Legs

(1) Ask the class to stay in their own personal floor space, going backwards and forwards within it, rather than all following one another round the outside of the room, being impeded by and impeding others.

(2) The timing of the arm swing to assist the jump needs lots of practice. Let the class feel the firm, strong, wide position while standing, before running and jumping to try it in flight.

(3) A shuttling, one way and back, running and jumping sequence needs little space. The 'explosive' drive up comes at the take-off, with knees bending and springing and the arm pulling up, rather than from a great, long run up.

Body

(1) This rhythmic, long, slow, swinging activity can be done by mirroring the teacher to start

with. Every joint alternately stretches and bends, and the arm swings lead the whole movement. Fingertips can brush the floor on the 'backwards, forwards, backwards swings'.

(2) When they understand it, let them swing at their own rhythm, which they may quietly say as they perform. 'One (as they swing arms up) two, three, four (bent and bouncing) and up.'

Arms

(1) Wide arms and legs are as they were in one of the jumps at the start. Straight arms are strong and safe. Emphasise this so that they are habitually straight when inverted or on hands and feet.

(2) Hands and feet close together is easier, physically, than when they are apart. It is possible to include some moments when all the weight is on the hands, as in a bunny jump forwards and on to hands only.

APPARATUS WORK

(1) Pursue good quality movement by praising and demonstrating with pupils whose walking, running, jumping, bouncing, skipping is neat, quiet, well controlled, never following others, and appropriate for the part of the room where they are doing it.

(2) Quiet feet, quiet pupils moving and listening for the teacher in a quiet voice to call 'Stop!', is a desirable tradition. This usually means a safe, well ordered environment and few stoppages.

(3) The quick reaction to the teacher's instruction is matched by the need for quick planning to decide which body part and new shape to use on the next 'Stop!' Ask for a firm,

strong, hard-working body in the held shape, with no lazy sagging.

(4) The runs and jumps on the floor can be adjusted to arrive on a mat, so that you are near a piece of apparatus to mount and travel on. Teacher commentary on actions which make good use of hands and feet support will expand the class repertoire.

(5) As in the floorwork, let the hands and feet travelling be slow, careful and thoughtful. As well as the straight, safe arms when weight is mainly on hands, emphasise the 'thumbs under' grip on bars for safety.

FINAL FLOOR ACTIVITY

This sequence includes good variety with its stillness at start and finish; its run and vigorous leap with strong body shape; and its slow, easy swinging on the spot.

Year 1 • November • Lesson 3

LESSON PLAN • 30 MINUTES

Emphasis on: (a) body parts awareness as you plan and carry out tasks; (b) pursuit of near non-stop, quiet, neat, thoughtful, focused activity, both in floorwork and in travelling up to, on and from apparatus.

FLOORWORK   12 minutes

Legs
(1) Can you show me a variety of ways you can travel, using one foot, both feet or one foot after the other?
(2) 'Variety' means more than one activity, i.e. using at least two different moves, such as skipping forwards, then two-footed bouncing sideways.
(3) Please travel along straight lines, never curving round or following others.
Body
(1) From different starting positions can you travel by going from body part to body part? (For example, from feet to knees, to seat, to lying on back, to shoulders.)

(2) How are you linking your positions together? (Lowering, sitting, rocking, twisting, stretching, rolling.)
(3) Can you include a hard-working, clear body shape at each position? (No lazy sagging.)
Arms
(1) Can you try a little bunny jump, keeping arms straight and knees bent?
(2) Fingers point forwards and arms are straight for a strong position.
(3) In a brilliant bunny jump your shoulders are above your hips, which are above your hands.

APPARATUS WORK   16 minutes

(1) Show me your favourite ways to travel on feet on the floor only, not touching any apparatus except the mats.
(2) Can you include some of the variety from your floorwork as you go under, over, across, along, or in and out of the apparatus, still without touching it? (A hop across a mat; a two-footed bounce astride a bench; walking and running often.)
(3) Now move on to the apparatus, visiting pieces that are not crowded. How many parts of your body can grip the apparatus as you travel on it? (Hands and feet climb on ropes and climbing frame; back of knees and hands grip under a pole; tummy and hands circle on a bar; hands only swing on a rope; hands pull along a plank; feet take you along benches, planks, boxes.)
(4) Can you arrive on the apparatus using your hands strongly to lift, twist, pull, lever, swing, roll you on? Make your feet important when you leave the apparatus.
(5) Go from apparatus to apparatus, touching each piece with hands only, and show me a bunny jump with straight arms and well bent legs.

FINAL FLOOR ACTIVITY   2 minutes

Stand with feet together and do an upward jump. Run forwards a very short distance (about 3 metres) and into a second jump. Use your stretched arms to help you balance in the air and on landing.

FLOORWORK

Legs

(1) Planning to include examples of travelling on one, two and alternate feet is a good challenge. The teacher will need to be observant in identifying and commenting on the varied examples if the class repertoire is to be extended.

(2) Ask half the class to observe the other half, and to look out for and name the actions seen, in order to share ideas. 'Variety' can be based on different actions, directions or body shapes (star jump different to tucked jump, for example).

(3) Lesson after lesson, we are after straight travelling into own spaces. Too often in primary schools, all follow each other anti-clockwise in a big circle.

Body

(1) With a less responsive or creative class, the teacher can lead them through a series of starting positions to get the activity going. We want a travel element and a still, held element that has good body tension and a neat appearance.

(2) Once again, the teacher can call out and suggest the links. 'From standing tall and still; all lower down to kneeling; rock back on to your seat; lower back to lying; now swing up on to shoulders.'

(3) Ask class to 'feel strong, with muscles firm.' Our bodies work harder and look neater when we make our shapes firm and clear.

Arms

(1) 'Show me your hands' will have whole class holding hands towards teacher, who checks that arms are straight with fingers pointing forwards: two important safety elements when inverted.

(2) Pupils crouch down and place the hands on the floor, under the shoulders. Body weight is forwards on flat hands and tips of toes.

(3) One or two little preparatory jumps off the floor with both feet precede the stronger push up on to hands.

APPARATUS WORK

(1) During this period, while the class is travelling freely without touching apparatus, the teacher can make last minute adjustments to the apparatus positions. Ensure that none is too near the side or end walls and that all mats are properly placed.

(2) Class are asked to plan examples of travelling on one, two and alternate feet, as already practised in the floorwork. Such travelling must be used as appropriate, as in the examples given.

(3) A lesson on 'body parts awareness' works the best, of course, when the class are challenged to support themselves, travel, climb, swing, balance and move on apparatus. In this lesson, their focus is on the body parts concerned.

(4) The focus now is on how to use your hands to bring, mount, swing, pull, lever or roll yourself on to the different pieces of apparatus. Feel the different actions taking place. Safe controlled steps, jumps or bounces are the focus in leaving the apparatus and 'making the feet important'.

(5) Children are sensible about how high they lift feet off the floor. The unsure do a tentative, low lift of feet and bent legs. The more confident make their bunny jumps go higher off the floor.

FINAL FLOOR ACTIVITY

Aware of feet in run and jump. Aware of arms in air and on landing. Aware of whole, still body at the start and finish.

LESSON PLAN • 30 MINUTES

Emphasis on: (a) body shape awareness, in stillness and motion; (b) improving the look of the work by making the body shape precise; (c) expressing pleasure in demonstrations by others, and picking out the main features in a demonstration.

FLOORWORK   12 minutes

Legs

(1) Can you run and jump up high with feet together and long, straight legs?

(2) Try one and two-footed take-offs to see which gives you the better jump upwards.

(3) When you land, use long, straight arms up, forwards or sideways to help your balance.

(4) Now run and jump high, showing a wide shape like a star, with arms and legs stretched wide.

Body

(1) Lie on your back, curled up small, with hands clasped under knees. Can you rock backwards and forwards, keeping your body curled and head on knees?

(2) Now, can you roll from side to side, still curled up small and round, with hands clasped under knees?

(3) Can you roll from side to side, then to the first side, and right over on to tummy and on to back again? To one side; to other side; to first side and right over.

Arms

(1) Start crouched on hands and feet, small and curled in. Travel to a long, stretched position, still on hands and feet, by moving hands or feet only. Move back to your crouch position by moving hands or feet only.

(2) With straight arms and legs in the travel, your body will be working very hard. Try it.

(3) Feel if it is harder to travel with straight arms and legs close together or wide apart.

APPARATUS WORK   16 minutes

(1) Run quietly round the room, not touching any apparatus. When I call 'Stop!', show me a clear body shape on the nearest piece of apparatus. 'Stop!' Are you really stretched, wide, curled or arched?

(2) Run round again. On my next signal, show me a new body shape on a different piece of apparatus. 'Stop!'

(3) Travel from apparatus to apparatus, putting hands only on each piece and jumping feet up off floor, as in a bunny jump. Show me strong, straight arms and well bent legs while on your hands.

(4) Travel freely on all the apparatus, showing me different actions as you move up to, on to, along and from the apparatus.

(5) In all your travelling, make your whole body shape clear and firm as you work hard to make your work look neater and better.

(6) Can you leave the apparatus sometimes with a high jump and a squashy landing, then a sideways roll on the mat, curled up like a little ball?

FINAL FLOOR ACTIVITY   2 minutes

Run and jump stretched; run and jump wide; then run and jump with own choice of body shape.

LESSON NOTES • 4 LESSONS DEVELOPMENT

FLOORWORK

Legs
(1) Because the jumping is the main activity, the run should only be for three or four strides. Discourage those who run all round the room (disturbing others) before doing their jump.

(2) An upward jump is more easily done from a two-footed take-off. Both feet are under you, driving upwards.

(3) In addition to improving the appearance of the work, straight arms act like a tightrope walker's pole, helping you to balance.

(4) Demonstrate with outstanding performers. Hard work is needed to achieve a wide shape in the short time the body is in flight.

Body
(1) Use step by step teaching to put them in the correct, curled starting position. 'Lie down on your back. Curl up small with your back rounded. Clasp your hands together under your knees. Put your head on your knees. Swing back and rock on to your shoulders. Now, swing forwards, back on to your seat.'

(2) The impetus for the sideways movement comes from the knees swinging to that side.

(3) The impetus for the complete roll over comes from a strong pull to that side by the bent legs and head.

Arms
(1) The class can mirror the teacher to place them all in the low, crouched starting position, with weight equally on hands and feet. They then have to plan their move to the contrasting stretched position, travelling on hands only or feet only.

(2) On straight arms and legs, our crouch position is more of an arch, demanding suppleness and strength.

(3) A high arch results from hands and feet being close together. A much lower arch (very hard to support) results from hands and feet being wider apart.

APPARATUS WORK

(1) This activity demands an immediate response to a signal, followed by quick decision-making on where to go to show a clear body shape. Praise those pupils who have found an excellent space to show an admirable, firm, clear, hard-working body shape.

(2) Ideally, the new body shape will also be performed on a new supporting body part, not always on feet which are most commonly used.

(3) The bunny jump was introduced last month and is here being practised for further improvement. It helps to take off from a starting position where feet are very near to the apparatus.

(4) From the 'one touch only and away' of the bunny jumps, they now linger and travel further on the apparatus, focusing first of all on the actions being performed. They should be thinking 'I am climbing, swinging, balancing, rolling, jumping, stepping, sliding, pulling, hanging, circling, lowering.'

(5) Their focus now should be on body shapes that are neat, correct, safe and attractive as they travel through the actions above.

(6) We have practised high jumps, squashy landings and sideways rolls, and are now trying to link them together smoothly.

FINAL FLOOR ACTIVITY

Two thirds of the activity are teacher-led. The pupils have to plan what their third activity will be. The whole sequence can be done round a small triangle.

Year 1 • January • Lesson 5

LESSON PLAN • 30 MINUTES

Emphasis on: (a) space awareness and the unselfish sharing of space with a concern for own and others' safety; (b) linking actions in a well planned way, and demonstrating enthusiastically when asked.

FLOORWORK   12 minutes

Legs

(1) Can you travel round the room using your feet, sometimes facing forwards and sometimes in another direction?

(2) You can try walking forwards, bouncing sideways, and, very carefully, skipping backwards.

(3) Are you looking for quiet parts of the room to go into each time?

Body

(1) Can you show me a still balance with part of your body stretched up to a high level?

(2) Now change to being on a different body part, with another part stretched high. (For example, from standing on tiptoes with one arm upstretched; to being on one foot and two hands with one leg upstretched; to being on seat with legs and arms upstretched.)

(3) Can you be very clever and join up two or three balances and stretches?

Arms

(1) Can you take your weight on your hands, lift your legs up into the air, then bring them down quietly in a new place?

(2) Pretend that the floor is a bench and you are taking your feet from one side to the other, while on your hands. You can try this later on the benches.

(3) Remember to keep your arms straight for a strong position, and your head looking forwards (not back under arms which makes everything appear upside down).

APPARATUS WORK   16 minutes

(1) As you travel on the floor and mats only, not touching any apparatus yet, can you visit every part of the room – the ends, sides, corners and middle?

(2) You may go under, across, along and in and out of the apparatus, but still no touching. Keep moving and looking for the quiet spaces where you will have lots of room.

(3) Use the floor and the apparatus to show me travelling where you are near to the apparatus. (For example, tight grip on ropes and climbing frames; pulling, sliding low along benches and planks; circling on metal poles and climbing frame bars; rolls on mats.)

(4) On feet only, travel up to and on to the apparatus. Show me a high stretched balance above the apparatus. Then do an upward jump off, followed by a squashy landing and a sideways roll on a mat.

(5) Can you arrive on and leave the apparatus at different places and in different ways?

FINAL FLOOR ACTIVITY   2 minutes

Run and jump to land facing a new direction.

36

FLOORWORK

Legs
(1) Demonstrate the meanings of 'Forwards; backwards, sideways' with a follow-the-leader start, all copying the teacher. Within that practice, ask for special care on the backwards movements which should not last long, for safety's sake.
(2) Demonstrations of varied ways to travel will quickly increase the class repertoire, as will suggestions by the teacher (who is, after all, teaching, as well as encouraging originality and drawing out ideas).
(3) Sometimes a 'quiet part' is the space where you are already. Stay there for a second or two if the floor ahead is busy. All the actions normally done on the move can also be done on the spot.
Body
(1) Define a 'balance' as 'When your body is held still on some small or unusual part, not wobbling because you are working hard to hold it steady.'

(2) While the stretched part is always extending high, the idea of working at different levels can be put across here. Each balance can be shown at a different level, i.e. high, medium or low.
(3) The whole sequence is done slowly, showing clearly the linking movements such as bending down; lowering to sitting; twisting on to a different part; rolling up on to shoulders.
Arms
(1) The idea of 'air space' in addition to floor space is being explained and put across here. Many of our gymnastic activities happen in the space above and around us. Much of the work also happens on our hands, which are often working as hard as our feet and legs, particularly on apparatus.
(2) 'Let's pretend...' helps to give a picture of the desired pattern.
(3) It is a good idea to ask them to hold the crouched, ready position for the teacher to check; straight arms; head looking forwards; fingers pointing forwards.

APPARATUS WORK

(1) Challenge the class to visit all parts of the room, weaving in and out of all the apparatus and sharing the space sensibly with others.
(2) The 'under, over, along, across, in and out of, through' inspires lots of interesting activity and a first-hand experience of the meaning of these prepositions.
(3) Class should use a variety of ways to hold on to (with arms and legs) and travel along (on, under, around or across) apparatus, in close proximity to each piece.

(4) In 'feet only' travelling, the ropes are out of bounds because you need both hands and feet on a rope. The majority of infant school apparatus is low (mats, benches, planks, parts of boxes) so that this task is easily worked at, with plenty of pieces for all to share. The 'travel; balance; jump; land; roll' is a good example of linking actions into gymnastic sequences.
(5) There is a dual challenge to plan for, namely to arrive on and leave the apparatus at different places, and to demonstrate different actions when mounting and leaving it.

FINAL FLOOR ACTIVITY

'Can you run and jump four times, and land facing a different side of the room each time?'

Year 1 • February • Lesson 6

LESSON PLAN • 30 MINUTES

Emphasis on: (a) jumping and landing, learning to absorb shock; (b) rolling; (c) repeating, practising, improving and remembering sequences of linked actions.

FLOORWORK   12 minutes

Legs

(1) Jump and land in your own floor space. Spring up with a good stretch in your ankles. Land softly and quietly by letting your ankles, knees and hips 'give' like springs.

(2) Use a short run, then jump up high from one or both feet. Feel your nice, squashy landing, with knees bending well.

(3) Let's join them together now. Do one jump on the spot, then do a very short run in to a second upward jump. Aim for a silent landing each time.

Body

(1) Lie on your back, curled up small, and roll backwards and forwards from your seat all the way to your shoulders.

(2) With your hands beside your shoulders, thumbs in, fingers out, push the floor while on your shoulders, to rock you back to sitting.

(3) With hands clasped under knees, still curled up on your back, can you roll smoothly from side to side?

(4) Lie on your back with your body straight. Can you twist to one side to roll over on to your front, then over on to your back again?

Arms

(1) Can you join together two or three bunny jumps on the spot with some travelling using hands and feet?

(2) Do all the movements slowly so that I can see clearly what your interesting actions are.

(3) Try to remember your actions exactly. (For example, hands only to walk forwards for 6 counts, then feet to bounce forwards for 4 counts.)

APPARATUS WORK   16 minutes

(1) As you travel all round the room, without touching any apparatus, can you include safe jumps across parts of mats, over benches and low planks?

(2) Working nearer the apparatus now, can you show me jumping movements, still without touching any apparatus? (For example, bouncing, feet astride and along benches or planks; jumping, feet together; weaving in and out of ropes; jumping from a standing start across a low barbox with a good arm swing to help you.)

(3) Jump and land on a mat, do a soft, squashy landing, then a sideways roll to bring you on to hands and feet. Jump up, and off you go again.

(4) Travel freely on floor and apparatus now. In your travelling, I would like to see your movements done slowly and clearly. With a nicely stretched body, can you jump up and off the apparatus, land softly and lower into a smooth, sideways roll?

(5) You may add in rolling on mats and rolling from apparatus. For example, rolling from sitting, kneeling, lying on benches, planks or low box tops. You choose. Roll forwards or sideways.

FINAL FLOOR ACTIVITY   2 minutes

Show me how softly and silently you can do four jumps to each side of the room in turn.

38

FLOORWORK

Legs

(1) Ankles are seldom stretched fully in everyday life, so many will be stiff. A demonstration by someone with strong, supple ankles is essential to show how to stretch beautifully on take-off and 'give' on landing.

(2) The short run will be of three or four strides only. Once again, we want to feel the ankles stretching as the driving force at take-off. A squashy landing is felt as the knees give.

(3) Sequences of linked actions can be as simple as this jump on the spot; then the run and jump; then the landing; plus, of course the still, upright, proud starting and finishing positions.

Body

(1) It helps the rolling to think of a body part that swings you in to the rolls. From being curled up on your back, the legs swing you forwards, and the upper body swings you backwards.

(2) The hands at shoulders position lets you practise the equivalent of the start of a backward roll from sitting, and the end of a forward roll from being on shoulders.

(3) Together, the knees and clasped hands swing you from side to side. Elbows in and head on chest keep you nicely rounded.

(4) A twist to roll to the right is started by the left leg or the left shoulder coming across. Some pupils dislike rolling on a rounded back, but don't mind doing it with a straight body.

Arms

(1) One lesson emphasis is the 'practising, improving and remembering' of sequences and linked movements. Two or three different actions and the associated one or two linking movements have to be planned and remembered to allow repetition.

(2) 'No quick scampering!', so that full, clear actions are being performed at a speed that calls for good strength and control.

(3) The teacher can say 'Pretend I am watching each one of you to see exactly what you are doing. Repeat your sequence, time after time, to help me.'

APPARATUS WORK

(1) The run and jump practices of the start of the lesson are now being practised to clear low apparatus carefully and only when you have a good space to land on.

(2) Instead of approaching, clearing and moving away from apparatus, we now stay near it, still practising jumping as we travel next to, along, or in and out of it.

(3) There will be nine or ten mats widely spaced about the room. We are now linking a run, jump, landing and a sideways roll, to be followed by a lively spring up on to both feet. Run away again, looking for the next clear mat.

(4) The mixture of travelling freely on all apparatus, particularly using hands and feet; jumping off with a nicely stretched body; landing softly, knees 'giving'; then rolling sideways, makes an attractive sequence of varied and contrasting activities.

(5) Rolls can start from on a piece of apparatus, in addition to the obvious starts from the side of a mat.

FINAL FLOOR ACTIVITY

Class activities where all work in unison are popular. This one has everybody starting facing the front and working round to each side, four by four.

Year 1 • March • Lesson 7

LESSON PLAN • 30 MINUTES

Emphasis on: (a) balance held with good body tension and a good body shape; (b) increasing self-confidence showing through in positive effort; (c) pleasure evident in enthusiastic participation.

FLOORWORK   12 minutes

Legs
(1) Stand tall and still. Now lift one foot off the floor and hold your balance by leaning to one side a little bit. Change feet and balance again.
(2) Travel about the hall on your feet in many ways. When I call 'Stop!', be perfectly balanced, still and on tiptoes.
(3) Now change to running a few steps, then jumping and landing in a beautifully balanced position, where your body is working hard to avoid wobbling. A stretching of both arms sideways or forwards will help your balance.

Body
(1) Can you make up a sequence of three stretched body shapes that are also balances because they are difficult to hold still? Move from one to the next, stretching and being still again.
(2) 'Balance' means being on small or unusual body parts. Are you planning to be on small as well as unusual parts? (For example, on one foot; tiptoes; seat; shoulders; elbows and knees; one hand and one foot; one knee and one hand; two hands.)
(3) The balance will look neater and your body will be working harder if your stretches are really strong and firm.

Arms
(1) Crouch down on hands and feet, with weight forward on your hands. Try two little bounces, lifting your feet off the floor a little way. Then, on three, push off strongly with both feet up to a good bunny jump position. Can you hold the balance on your hands for two or three counts?
(2) Keep both arms straight, hands pointing forwards and head looking forwards to help your position and your balance.
(3) If you want to try a handstand balance, do it with your swinging up leg going well forwards, and the kicking leg staying back.

APPARATUS WORK   16 minutes

(1) There are many low pieces of apparatus spaced around the hall. Travel up to a piece and jump over it to land and hold a balance for a second or two before moving on to a new piece.
(2) Spacing out well, run round, using the floor only. When I call 'Stop!', show me a still, firm balance on the nearest piece of apparatus.
(3) When I stop you next time, show me a balance on a different body part on a new piece of apparatus. Can we have less balancing on feet only? 'Stop!'
(4) From a still starting position away from apparatus, travel up to and on to a piece of apparatus, and show me a still, beautifully stretched balance for two or three counts. Then leave the apparatus to finish in a neat, still position. Repeat up to and on to a new piece.
(5) Spend more time now staying and travelling on pieces of apparatus. Within your travelling, please let me see how often you can be in a strong, firm balance on different body parts.

FINAL FLOOR ACTIVITY   2 minutes

Balance, standing on one foot, body steady. Now change to the other foot and hold body steady but in a different position to the first balance.

FLOORWORK

Legs

(1) This simple balance can help the class to feel how hard their bodies work to remain still when balanced on a smaller part than usual. Arms will stretch sideways and the body will lean to the opposite side almost automatically to help keep balance.

(2) If they stop, standing on two feet as normal, no balance is involved. Emphasise the 'stretched, still balance on tiptoes' to make it a challenging balance.

(3) Once again, the still position at the end of the landing has to be on the balls of the feet to make it a balance. The feet can be apart, one in front of the other or side by side; or they can be together, which is a difficult balance.

Body

(1) Introduce this activity with the challenge 'Show me a beautifully stretched balance position, standing on tiptoes. Now lift one foot off the floor and balance on the other foot, still showing me an excellent, stretched, whole body shape.' Then ask class to start finding other body parts to hold a still, stretched balance on.

(2) As well as the standing start positions suggested by the teacher, the class can think about having front, back or side towards the floor, or being upended, as on shoulders. (Half of class watching and commenting on the supporting parts used by the other half demonstrating will add to class repertoire.)

(3) Say 'In your balance, let your body sag and be lazy. Now, let's do it properly and firm up the whole body. Really stretch the parts not being used to support you. Feel the difference.'

Arms

(1) Practice gets them to feel how much effort to put into a push from feet on to hands. Bent legs lift up quite easily.

(2) Demonstrate with good performers to explain 'Arms straight and head looking forwards' for a strong, safe, compact position.

(3) In the handstand, the one leg far forwards and one leg back almost make a straight line. This helps the balance like the long pole of the tightrope walker.

APPARATUS WORK

(1) This is like the third activity of the floorwork with a low obstacle to force a high jump. We want a balanced landing, ideally on the balls of the feet, with arms stretched firmly.

(2) Do not allow wandering to balance on a favourite piece. They must go straight to the nearest, and plan and decide quickly how and where to balance.

(3) Unless taught otherwise, the majority will simply stand semi-balanced on their feet. We want them to try holding a firm, nicely stretched balance on lower legs, seat, shoulders, one hand and one foot (front, back or side to floor), tummy, elbow and hand.

(4) A starting position; travel; mounting and balancing on apparatus; dismounting; and going to a finish position on the floor, all add up to an interesting and varied sequence of seven parts.

(5) Travelling on a variety of supporting parts alternates with balancing on a variety of parts. This provides variety and contrast, two important features of good sequences.

FINAL FLOOR ACTIVITY

The upper body can lean to one side or horizontally forwards, or be arched backwards

Year 1 • April • Lesson 8

LESSON PLAN • 30 MINUTES

Emphasis on: (a) working harder for longer, linking two or more simple actions to plan and create sequences; (b) demonstrating an expanding repertoire of well controlled, neat body movements.

FLOORWORK   12 minutes

Legs
(1) Using a still start and finish each time, can you show me a short sequence of favourite ways to travel using feet only?
(2) Can you name the two or three different actions you are including and remembering?
(3) Can you include varied actions (not always running and jumping) performed in a variety of ways (e.g. using different directions, shapes, speeds)?

Body
(1) Try to join together two or three arched, bridge-like shapes.
(2) This shape will have three or four sides, one of which is usually the floor.

(3) Please try a high bridge, like standing with your upper body reaching down. Then try bridges at a medium level (e.g. crab arch) and a low level (e.g. lying on your back with an arch between shoulders and heels).

Arms
(1) Plan to show me an interesting pathway as you travel using both hands and feet.
(2) You can go forwards and backwards to the same place; or round three sides of a triangle; or, if you are feeling strong and full of ideas, round four sides of a square.
(3) The variety and contrast, which is pleasing to see, can come from a change of direction, body shape or level (e.g. high cartwheels and low travel on hands and feet).

APPARATUS WORK   16 minutes

(1) Stand on the floor, perfectly still. Travel up to your nearest piece of apparatus using feet only; travel on to and along the apparatus, using both hands and feet; somewhere show me a bridge-like shape on your apparatus; leave the apparatus and return to a still finish position on the floor. Practise this sequence several times at the same piece of apparatus, so that you can remember and improve it.
(2) I would like to see a jump and a squashy landing somewhere. This could be on to a mat before you go on to the other apparatus, or it could be our way of leaving the apparatus. You might even include a sideways roll after the landing.

(3) All move to a new piece of apparatus and stand still, ready to start again. Remember to show me your best still start and finish positions, as well as your travelling; your making a bridge; and your jumping and landing. Stay at your present apparatus to practise, improve and remember your sequence.
(4) As well as the neat, still start and finish positions, I am looking for neat, quiet, well controlled actions; good, clear body shapes; and a change of direction or level somewhere for variety and contrast.

FINAL FLOOR ACTIVITY   2 minutes

Using feet only, show me a still, well stretched balance. Travel a few steps into a different balance. Travel to a third, different balance.

FLOORWORK

Legs

(1) 'Short' means two or three, so that the whole sequence is short enough to be remembered, but long enough to be interesting to do.

(2) Re-inforce the thoughtful planning by asking some of the class to name their actions, then demonstrate them.

(3) Varied actions could be hopping on one foot; bouncing on both feet; and jumping from one to both feet.

Body

(1) If the class are asked to point out some examples of bridge-like shapes in the room, they will more clearly understand the kind of shape that is wanted.

(2) If responses are slow, the teacher can lead the class through a bridge on two feet, with upper body bent forwards and down; then a bridge on one hand and one foot side towards the floor; then seated with the 'bridge' under both knees.

(3) The high arch on feet can be to the front, rear or either side. If a crab is too hard, they can have their front towards the floor, on hands and feet.

Arms

(1) Depending on the space available and whether they wish to practise two or more different actions, they will work on a straight line or a larger figure.

(2) 'A different action for each part of your two, three or four-sided figure, done slowly and in control' is the challenge.

(3) Decide on the actions first, making the body parts work neatly, in good control. Next, make the shapes firm and clear, particularly any stretches that work the body strongly. A change of direction to the side or zig-zagging, and/or a change of level, are always signs of thoughtful, versatile work.

APPARATUS WORK

(1) Pupils can stay at the apparatus they brought out as an easy way to ensure equal numbers everywhere. Their forward planning is being called on to work out: (a) their pathway from the starting position on floor to apparatus, and to finishing position on floor; (b) how and where they will travel throughout; (c) where it is appropriate to include the still, bridge-like shape.

(2) Still at the same apparatus, now add the jump and landing, and the opportunity to include a roll. To ensure that the work is focused and thoughtful, pupils might be forewarned 'In a minute or two I will ask for volunteers to demonstrate the sequences you have been practising, improving and remembering.'

(3) On alternate weeks they can move clockwise and anti-clockwise to the next piece of apparatus. Ensure variety by aiming to visit three groups each lesson. By organising groups to demonstrate the sharing of floor and apparatus space, and their near non-stop work, we show examples of what can be achieved at apparatus places still to be visited.

(4) Ample praise should be given for good effort at this difficult and challenging level of work being asked for.

FINAL FLOOR ACTIVITY

An A...B...C... pattern sequence with each of the three parts different and taking very little space.

LESSON PLAN • 30 MINUTES

Emphasis on: (a) partner work as a valuable contribution to learning to work co-operatively; (b) developing the ability to observe and recognise another's actions; (c) making appreciative comments and judgements on another's performance.

FLOORWORK   12 minutes

Legs
(1) Follow your leader round the room, travelling on feet only. Keep about 2 metres behind your partner so that you can see the foot and leg actions clearly.
(2) Leader, can you do more than one action for your partner to see and copy?
(3) Can you travel almost mirroring each other's actions, shapes and directions?

Body
(1) Show each other a favourite balance where part of your body is stretched strongly.
(2) Can you do these two balances slowly and carefully, one after the other, working together?

(3) Is it possible to make a gentle contact, with the stretched body parts touching each time?

Arms
(1) Let's have a new leader this time. (Follower at start of leg activity.) Take your partner travelling on hands and feet, with two or three interesting, favourite actions.
(2) Lead very slowly, maybe travelling a short distance, then waiting for your partner to observe and catch up.
(3) For variety, try changing direction or letting a different body part lead.

APPARATUS WORK   16 minutes

(1) Follow your leader up to, over, across, along, under, or in and out of apparatus, without touching anything other than mats. Keep about 2 metres apart, going along non-stop; or leader goes ahead and stops while partner watches, then catches up.
(2) With great care, new leader, show your partner a run and jump to bring you on to a mat, or to take you over a piece of very low apparatus.
(3) Now the leader will show you how to arrive on a piece of apparatus using hands only, and

how to leave, carefully using feet only. Take your time and wait until you have plenty of space, particularly if you are jumping off, landing and then rolling.
(4) Start in a floor space at opposite sides of your piece of apparatus, and about 3 or 4 metres away from it. Together, travel up to and on to the apparatus, pass each other carefully, and finish in your partner's starting place.

FINAL FLOOR ACTIVITY   2 minutes

Stand facing each other. With a little bending of the knees as a starting signal, can you bounce on the spot at exactly the same speed, mirroring each other?

FLOORWORK

Legs

(1) Emphasise that a good leader looks after the following partner by keeping his or her eyes open for good spaces to travel through, and by staying on straight lines, not curving around following everyone else. By stopping the class often to check that pairs are reasonably together and well spaced, the teacher can comment positively on good examples of leadership for others to observe and copy.

(2) Two or three different actions continually being repeated makes an interesting sequence if the couples are together.

(3) You watch your partner's actions first. Then you watch the shapes that are firm and clear. Then you hope for a change of direction at some point to add variety to the performance.

Body

(1) One watches while the other performs. Then they change duties. The observer looks to see which body parts are supporting and which are strongly stretched to enhance the appearance.

(2) After several practices, they move on to performing the two balances one after the other, both finishing in the held position.

(3) In the held position, they now make a gentle contact between the body parts stretching. They need to plan their starting relationship to ensure that a contact happens easily.

Arms

(1) Well spaced out to start with, couples should remain in their own parts of the room, working round a triangle or square shape.

(2) Travel; stop. Partner following ensures that the leader thinks about the actions, and leader ensures that the follower watches to copy. This is better than silly scampering, chasing one after the other.

(3) Variety in actions might be difficult to plan, but the variety inherent in changing direction and leading parts will help.

APPARATUS WORK

(1) They will prefer following non-stop, therefore the leader must go slowly and never become mixed up with other couples. Remind the leaders 'If it suddenly becomes crowded, stop your travelling, and your following partner should stop with you.'

(2) Waiting sometimes before the run and the jump will be essential to avoid bumps and accidents, as all share the nine or ten mats in a typical layout.

(3) Follower stands and watches partner's method of mounting the apparatus, making the hands important. While follower comes on to apparatus, the leader waits. Leader leaves the apparatus, making feet important, while follower observes only. Follower comes from apparatus and they finish at a place from which they start again, either at the same apparatus, or towards another piece.

(4) Coming towards the sides of a plank, bench, box or climbing frame, there will be plenty of room to pass each other, side by side. If they are coming along the length of a bench, plank, pole or on the same trestle, one should pause while the other tries to negotiate the still partner.

FINAL FLOOR ACTIVITY

The 'One, two, three, four' count of their feet on the floor should be felt leading them at just the right speed.

Year 1 • June • Lesson 10

LESSON PLAN • 30 MINUTES

Emphasis on: (a) swinging as an aid and impetus to movement; (b) making the hall a 'scene of busy activity', inspired by an enthusiastic attitude to participation.

FLOORWORK   12 minutes

Legs

(1) Stand with your knees slightly bent and both arms stretched behind you. Can you swing your arms forwards and up to help an upward jump on the spot?

(2) Do three of these jumps, all facing the same way, without stopping, letting your arms swing well backwards and forwards each time. Feel how your arms seem to pull you up.

(3) Stand with your knees slightly bent and one arm raised to one side at about hip height. Can you swing this arm into a jump to face the next side of the room? Do this four times back to your starting place, then try it round the other way, using the other arm to swing you.

Body

(1) Lie on your back, curled up small with your hands clasped under your knees. Your chin is on your chest so that you are curled from seat to head. Swing from side to side into sideways rolls, and feel which part your body is helping by its swinging action.

(2) Sit, curled up again. This time your hands are next to your shoulders. Rock back on to your hands, then push forwards on to your seat again. Can you feel how your head, then your feet help the movement by swinging you backwards and forwards?

(3) Lie stretched out on your back, hands by your sides. To help you to roll on to your front, swing with the opposite leg or shoulder, or both together.

Arms

(1) Can you swing up on to your hands? Try a swing of both arms from a start above your head, keeping them straight.

(2) Try to swing the kicking leg up behind you. Remember to keep looking forwards so that everything looks normal, not upside down, as it does if you look back under the arms.

(3) You choose now. Use the swinging method you found the best, and practise your handstands carefully.

APPARATUS WORK   16 minutes

(1) Can you do a short run and swing into an upward jump on to a mat or any of the low apparatus? You should feel the swing coming from an arm or a leg. You can swing up and from the apparatus, using both arms as we did at the very start of the lesson.

(2) Continue with this practice, but you may now add in a roll on a mat with a curled or a stretched body that swings to one side. Then you jump up, and off you go again.

(3) Now visit low pieces of apparatus, including mats, and put your hands on each piece with fingers pointing forwards and arms straight. Can you swing one leg up behind you to put all your weight on your hands for a second or two?

(4) Practise freely on all the apparatus and try to include: (a) a swing on to and from apparatus; (b) a swing into a roll; (c) a swing up to take all the weight on your hands.

FINAL FLOOR ACTIVITY   2 minutes

Follow your leader's travelling and swinging into a jump.

LESSON NOTES • 4 LESSONS DEVELOPMENT

FLOORWORK

Legs
(1) A demonstration by the teacher of the starting hands and knees positions and the lively upward swing will get the lesson off to a busy start.

(2) The stretched arms should feel strong at the end of the swing and be working as hard as the legs to give the whole body an attractive, well controlled look. The gentle 'give' in the knees and ankles on landing should be asked for and demonstrated.

(3) Left arm swings to right to make a quarter turn that is easily controlled, even when coming off apparatus later.

Body
(1) A really good, swinging, sideways roll can take you right over on to your front, then on to your back again.

(2) This practice gives a feel for the start of a backward roll and the end of a forward roll.

(3) Many pupils do not like rolling on a curled back, but do not mind rolling with a straight body. The swinging pull of the parts that start the action is very obvious when the body is straight.

Arms
(1) This long lever swing, with both arms starting above the head, is very strong and liable to make them overswing. Some like it.

(2) This lesser lever swing of the foot kicking up behind is easier to control and the hands are down near the floor to start with.

(3) Let them decide. The one they choose will be the one they use for practice from now on. Both methods have their supporters.

APPARATUS WORK

(1) There are lots of low surfaces, including mats, to share and work on. The little run adds to the force of the eventual swing. They are now thinking of, focusing on and planning to use swings to aid their jumps on to and up and from the various apparatus.

(2) Ideally, the sideways roll will come after a squashy landing from the jump up and off apparatus. It should form part of the landing, expanding their work by giving it variety and contrast.

(3) This is half way between a bunny jump and a handstand. Hands start on the apparatus, but only one leg does the swinging up behind action. If they wish to twist to come down on a

new floor space, there will be a little swing to that side by the legs and hips.

(4) The combination of mounting, travelling along and leaving apparatus, including a roll and weight on hands at some point, makes this a nicely varied sequence for them to practise, improve and then be asked to demonstrate. 'Observers, look out for and tell me where you could really see the swinging that helped to make these excellent sequences' and 'Performers, thank you very much for your non-stop, varied and exciting actions. Can any of you tell me where you felt the swing helping you the most?'

FINAL FLOOR ACTIVITY

Encourage them to choose a different partner to the one they worked with in the previous month's lesson. If the leader does a short run, then swings up into a jump to turn to face where they started from, they will need little space.

Year 1 • July • Lesson 11

LESSON PLAN • 30 MINUTES

Emphasis on: (a) sequences, and remembering and being able to repeat two or three simple actions to create a smooth, flowing performance; (b) arousing pleasure and a sense of fun from participation in vigorous and challenging activity.

FLOORWORK   12 minutes

Legs
(1) Using your legs only, can you make up a short sequence of your favourite ways to travel? Include a still start and finish.
(2) Variety will come from different sorts of actions, from different ways to use your body parts, and from changes of direction.
(3) If I watch you only, will I see the same two or three actions being repeated?
Body
(1) Show me how you can go from a favourite, still body shape on to a different body part, then into a different shape or back to the same one.
(2) Perform slowly so that I can see the linking movements clearly. (For example, roll, twist, lean, swing, jump, lower.)

(3) I hope all your shapes are firm and clear with no lazy, sagging bodies, please!
Arms
(1) As you travel on hands only, or on hands and feet, can you plan to show me an interesting pathway like a triangle or a square?
(2) Once again, if I am watching you only, will I see a starting and a finishing position where you are standing still?
(3) Variety can come from having back, side or front towards the floor; from different body shapes and directions; and from having different body parts leading the actions.

APPARATUS WORK   16 minutes

(1) Use a simple step or jump to bring you on to a piece of apparatus. With a beautifully stretched body, step or jump off on to a mat, do a soft, squashy landing, then a smooth sideways roll. Now move to a new piece of apparatus.
(2) Can you use your hands to lift, pull, lever or twist you on to the apparatus? Travel on the apparatus using hands and feet with varied actions, shapes and directions. As you leave the

apparatus, make your hands important this time.
(3) For the last apparatus part of our last lesson of the year, work freely at favourite ways of travelling on floor and apparatus. You can stay at one favourite piece, or use more than one piece, remembering the main actions on each so that you could repeat them for me. Off you go!

FINAL FLOOR ACTIVITY   2 minutes

Run and jump high with a stretched body shape. Run and jump high with a wide body shape. Run and jump high with your own choice of body shape, which might be stretched or wide again.

FLOORWORK

Legs

(1) 'Short sequence' infers a still, well controlled start; two or three linked and different ways to travel; and a still, neat finish position, so they do not need much space in which to perform.

(2) 'Using feet' with variety can mean feet together, separate or on one foot only; with straight, semi bent or well bent legs; on tiptoes, balls of foot or heels; walking, running, jumping, hopping, bouncing or skipping.

(3) A demonstration, with half watching half, can have the observers looking for a short, repeating pattern of two or three actions which they can identify.

Body

(1) As a reminder, the teacher can lead them through all the different shapes we normally see in gymnastic activities. 'Show me how you can go' challenges them to show good linking actions between the different shapes, moving from body part to body part.

(2) A three part sequence will be long enough for variety and to challenge their planning of different supporting parts and links.

(3) Words such as 'Strong, firm, clear, beautifully stretched and hard working' should be used in praising and encouraging good work.

Arms

(1) Each side of the triangle or square is only 2–3 metres, long enough to show the action two or three times before changing to the next one.

(2) Encourage a standing, still position when starting and finishing to signal 'I have done it once through' before repeating it.

(3) We want them to understand the pattern of thinking when planning for variety: What actions? What are body parts doing? What shapes am I showing clearly? Where am I doing it? In which directions?

APPARATUS WORK

(1) Up to, on to and almost immediately off the apparatus, with more time spent on the floor than on apparatus. The jump, land, sink to floor and roll sideways is the main part of the sequence, and there should be lots of potential demonstrators to call up.

(2) Using hands to mount, now spend more time on the apparatus, travelling in a thoughtful, well planned way which, ideally, you can remember and repeat.

(3) The year's teaching will have been successful if the class use this final part of the apparatus work to demonstrate: (a) quiet, almost non-stop, vigorous activity, performed with great enthusiasm; (b) an unselfish, considerate sharing of the space in the interest of own and others' safety; (c) neat, well controlled, versatile movements done wholeheartedly; (d) a sense of improved self-confidence due to the many achievements easily seen and recognised.

FINAL FLOOR ACTIVITY

One of the most marked improvements of the year will be their ability to show good quality running, jumping and landing; to make clear body shapes; and to hold a still starting and finishing position.

Year 2 • September • Lesson 1

LESSON PLAN • 30 MINUTES

Emphasis on: (a) unselfish co-operation in sharing floor and apparatus space; (b) immediate responses to instructions; (c) variety in travelling on floor and apparatus, using feet, feet and hands, and other body surfaces.

FLOORWORK · 12 minutes

Legs

(1) Can you walk, run, jump and land without stopping, and carry on with your walking again?

(2) Because you are travelling non-stop, look ahead and plan to walk, then run just the right distance to let you do your lively jump in a good space.

(3) Can you show me other ways to travel, using legs only? (For example, skip, bounce, gallop, hopscotch, slip sideways.)

Body

(1) Lie down on your back, front or side. Stretch your body out fully, reaching your arms above your head and pointing your toes. Can you travel by changing to a curled shape? Try it again. (For example, to lying curled on one side after sideways roll.)

(2) From your bent shape, can you now travel to a new supporting part, with your body stretched again? (For example, roll on to knees, stretch arms forwards and up above head.)

(3) Now can you do one more curl and stretch for me? (For example, roll to a sitting, curled position, then rock back to stretched shoulder balance.) Go back to your starting position and try again.

Arms

(1) Look for a clear space each time, then travel slowly on hands and feet. Try to show me your actions clearly.

(2) Are you sometimes using hands and feet apart, and sometimes closer together? Which way is easier?

(3) Can you travel by moving hands only and then feet only, stretching, then curling your body?

APPARATUS WORK · 16 minutes

(1) Using feet only, travel to all parts of the room where you see good spaces, but do not touch any apparatus.

(2) Can you do your floorwork, walking, running and jumping without stopping? (For example, walking across, under, through, in and out of apparatus; running on floor, across mats, astride benches; jumping over mats, benches, low planks.)

(3) Use your feet only to bring you on to, take you along, then bring you off the apparatus. Plan to show me a good variety of actions. (For example, step, jump or bounce on; walk, skip, bounce, run, hop along; then step, bounce or high jump from.)

(4) Now you may use both hands and feet to take you travelling up to, on, along and from the apparatus. Travel slowly enough for me to see your different actions clearly.

(5) Earlier, in our floorwork, we travelled by going from a stretch to a curl. Can you now travel on floor and all apparatus, changing from a long, stretched body to one that is curled up small? (For example, up and down the climbing frames; on two ropes with a stretched swing to a curled landing; under and on poles, planks, benches and boxes; rolling across mats.)

FINAL FLOOR ACTIVITY · 2 minutes

Show me one way to travel, using your feet silently.

50

FLOORWORK

Legs
(1) Pupils will jump, land and be still, if it is not emphasised that we 'Land and keep going!'
(2) The jump is the main feature, and some pupils will need to be dissuaded from running long distances without a jump.
(3) Much teacher commentary on activities observed and selected demonstrations will inspire the variety aimed for in this lesson.

Body
(1) It helps to produce a quick response if the teacher suggests a starting, stretched position from which it is easy to curl up.
(2) If class are slow to respond, the teacher once again can suggest a next move which satisfies the set task.
(3) From needing an assisted start to the sequence, the class, week by week, will begin to introduce their own ideas for supporting parts, and even include different levels.

Arms
(1) Insist on 'Slow travelling, using both hands and feet. No quick scampering!' Rushing around in and out of one another is common, but puts little weight on hands and does little to build skill, strength or understanding.
(2) 'Hands and feet apart' can mean a cartwheel, as well as the travel with hands and feet both supporting down near the floor. Wide hands and feet, with a long body near to floor, is difficult to support. Hands and feet close in a high arch is also difficult.
(3) You can have front (the usual), back or one side to the floor, as you move hands only, then feet only.

APPARATUS WORK

(1) Travel everywhere, except on apparatus. To test their 'immediate responses' and their 'unselfish sharing of floor', the teacher can call 'Stop!' Praise those who respond immediately and those who are in a space, well away from others.
(2) With good planning and thinking ahead, they can travel non-stop, walking, running and jumping as appropriate.
(3) 'Feet only travelling' means that we cannot use ropes, and can only step on and off the climbing frames from a low height. Praise neat, quiet actions with good body shapes and good use of arms for any balancing from jumps.
(4) 'Hands and feet travelling now' brings all apparatus into use. Discourage queues at favourite ropes and climbing frames, and encourage a continuous circulation from piece to adjacent piece.
(5) Revision of the floorwork, plus new work now possible on floor and apparatus, will challenge their planning ability as they climb, roll, swing, circle, vault, travel, while thinking about their changing body shapes. It will also challenge the teacher to be aware of what is going on and to comment on and demonstrate it, if it seems good addition to the class repertoire.

FINAL FLOOR ACTIVITY

The teacher can say 'If I close my eyes and ask you to travel on your feet so silently that I cannot hear you, what action or actions will you choose to use?'

LESSON PLAN • 30 MINUTES

Emphasis on: (a) controlling the body shape to enhance the appearance of a performance and to make you work harder; (b) observing demonstrations with interest, and describing the actions enjoyed and any special features.

FLOORWORK   12 minutes

Legs

(1) Stand tall and still on tiptoes. Run and jump up into a beautifully stretched jump with straight arms high above head. Land softly and show a still, tall finish.

(2) Try one and two-footed take-offs to see which gives you more height and time to make your big stretch in the air.

(3) You can land with feet apart, side to side, or one in front of the other. Or you can land with one foot after the other, which slows you down nicely for your neat, still finish. On landing, feel how straight arms help your balance.

Body

(1) Can you keep at least one hand on the floor and show me how to join together different body movements and shapes, such as bending, stretching, twisting and arching?

(2) If you are short of ideas, lie on your back with hands on the floor and body wide stretched. Now come up to sitting curled; change to side, falling stretched on one hand and one foot; put the top (non-supporting) hand under the other arm and twist to lie on back again.

(3) I will find your linking movements interesting. Show me slowly and clearly how you change from shape to shape.

Arms

(1) With one, both or alternate hands on the floor, can you lift your legs in the air, stretching them long and high?

(2) Your arms will also be long and straight for a safe, strong support.

APPARATUS WORK   16 minutes

(1) Run silently in and out of one another without touching any apparatus except mats. When I call 'Stop!', show me a clear, still body shape on the nearest apparatus. 'Stop!'

(2) When I stop you next time, try to show me a body shape that contrasts with one of the others on the apparatus with you.

(3) Travel up to your first piece of apparatus and arrive on it with your body curled up strongly. (For example, hanging from pole, rope or plank; crouched small on feet on climbing frames, box top; curled on shoulders on mats, planks, box; lying on one side on plank, box,

mat.) From this still start, change to travelling on your apparatus and try to include clear body shapes as you go. After you leave the apparatus, show me a still, tall, stretched finishing position.

(4) Stay at your number one apparatus and show me a sequence that includes: (a) strong leg and arm travelling actions; (b) varied body movements – bending, stretching, curling, twisting; (c) a variety of clear body shapes, both still and moving; (d) a still starting and finishing position on the floor away from the apparatus.

FINAL FLOOR ACTIVITY   2 minutes

How many travelling actions can you do with a leg or legs nicely stretched?

FLOORWORK

Legs

(1) Good posture and tall, erect, unsagging carriage are commented on right from start of the lesson. A wholehearted effort is needed to produce this clearly stretched, whole body shape in flight - and wholeheartedness is always one of our aims.

(2) Only a short, 3-4 metre run is needed to prepare you for the settle and upward spring, which is strongest from both feet.

(3) A slow, controlled landing is easier if feet land one after the other, slowing you down gradually. Straight arms forwards or sideways act to balance you.

Body

(1) The body movement part of the floorwork is often the most difficult to get started, because the actions and movements are unusual and not often experienced. All the more important,

therefore, to encourage these big body movements in order to retain our whole body suppleness and strength.

(2) A directed start by the teacher helps the class to understand the task and gives them starting points from which to develop their own ideas during future lessons.

(3) All sequences of joined up movements need linking actions. Skill in linking actions is as admirable and worth praising as good performances of the main movements.

Arms

(1) Ensure that all have good space behind them to let them kick up a leg into their cartwheels or handstands. The kicking up leg is straight and stays stretched during the move.

(2) Straight arms tend to stay unbending and strong. Any 'give' in the arm while upended can easily cause a collapse.

APPARATUS WORK

(1) Encourage running 'in and out of one another', to and from all directions, rather than all following all in one big circle. The 'Stop!' lets the teacher check on the quality of their spacing and their immediate response to a signal.

(2) If there are four or five sharing a set of apparatus, the one you choose to contrast with might in turn be concentrating on another. We hope to see a variety of supporting body parts, not always the easy support on feet, or hands and feet.

(3) A stationary start on the floor is followed by a travel up to and a stationary, held, curled body position on your first piece of apparatus. Pupils

then stay on and travel on the apparatus, trying to emphasise changing body shapes as they go.

(4) 'Number one apparatus' means the group which a team brought out. Teams should be reasonable in size, and start off by standing on the floor, 3–4 metres away from their apparatus. This starting signal is matched by a similar finishing signal after including all the parts in the challenge. (Groups rotate clockwise and anti-clockwise in alternate lessons, aiming to visit three or four sets of apparatus in any one lesson. All sets of apparatus will be visited at least once per fortnight.)

FINAL FLOOR ACTIVITY

Leaping, hurdling, high bouncing, jumping, walking, hopping, hopscotch, slipping sideways.

Year 2 • November • Lesson 3

Emphasis on: (a) space awareness, and the unselfish sharing and good use of it (directions, levels, own and general space); (b) linking movements with obvious control and understanding.

FLOORWORK   12 minutes

Legs

(1) In your own small floor space, can you run with high knee lifts? Then show me your choice of ways to travel, using legs and covering the whole floor space.

(2) In your travelling all round the room, can you plan to follow the same pathway each time?

(3) Can you include a direction change somewhere? Don't always travel forwards.

Body

(1) Can you join together three bridge-like shapes, supporting yourself perfectly still each time on different body parts?

(2) You can stand, kneel or lie, and your back, front or side can be towards the floor. You might even be upended on shoulders.

(3) It would be very good to see two or more different levels, please. (For example, high on tiptoes, body angled down; medium crab; low sitting or lying.)

Arms

(1) Can you take your body weight on to one, two or alternate hands, take your legs up into the air space above your head, then bring them down to a different floor space?

(2) Handstanders can take legs high into the space. If you are happier doing lower bunny jumps, remember to plan to move your feet to a different finishing place on the floor.

(3) Slow and quiet movements will look best. Keep your arm or arms straight for a safe, strong support.

APPARATUS WORK   16 minutes

(1) Touching only the floor and mats to start with, can you show me some running or bouncing in your own floor space; include some neat, travelling actions to take you across, along, round, under or in and out of the apparatus without touching any.

(2) From a still start in a floor space each time, can you plan ways to travel up to, on to, along and from the apparatus with a change of direction somewhere?

(3) Touching apparatus with hands only, take your weight on your hands with straight arms and bent legs. Can you bring your feet down softly in a new floor space?

(4) Use all the apparatus as you travel freely about the room. Plan to show me different levels at which you can travel and hold a still position on the apparatus. (For example, travel high on climbing frames; roll low across mats or pull along benches; walk in a medium crab arch; hold a high stand on a box top; a medium arch on a plank, or a low body close to a bench or mat.)

FINAL FLOOR ACTIVITY   2 minutes

Plan and show me a pattern of movements which include an action on the spot, followed by movements where you travel forwards, sideways, backwards or diagonally.

FLOORWORK

Legs

(1) Work in your own space for about eight running steps, knees high and arms working strongly to balance legs. Then travel about the whole space, planning to make a pathway that you can remember and repeat. For example, an oval, circle, triangle or figure of eight.

(2) Because they are following the same pathway in the whole room space, they might need to perform their travel action on the spot sometimes if they see a crowd ahead of them, impeding progress.

(3) Be very careful if travelling backwards. Look over one shoulder.

Body

(1) They can be asked to identify any bridge-like shapes in the room as a guide to their arched shape making.

(2) Demonstrations and teacher comment on the varied possible supporting parts are necessary to increase the class repertoire. Some of the arches can be very small, such as that below knees while sitting, or below body while on elbows and knees.

(3) Changing levels requires good linking movements – sitting, twisting, lowering, springing, rolling, rocking, tilting.

Arms

(1) Ask class to look at a mark on the floor where they are standing at the start. Their next take-off spot will be from a new mark.

(2) They can pretend to be taking weight on hands on a low box top, and coming down on the opposite side, often by twisting hips and legs against the fixed hands.

(3) 'Slow' gives the impression of everything being under control. A still, erect starting and finishing position also enhances the appearance of the work.

APPARATUS WORK

(1) A repeat of the starting leg activity, but with the need to plan ahead to negotiate apparatus.

(2) Sideways travel on most apparatus is easy, particularly if moving on hands and feet. A jump up sideways from bench, low box or planks is done carefully and when there is plenty of space.

(3) The teacher can say 'Show me your hands and straight arms ' as class hold arms forwards. Fingers should be spread and to the front, and arms in the strong, straight and safe position they will use. Short lever, bent legs lift up more quickly than legs kept straight. On some apparatus, hands are flat on top. On others, they grip the sides. On ropes, hands are close together, gripping. On climbing frames, one hand will be gripping a bar higher than the other hand.

(4) The message is probably 'On and hold; travel and hold; travel and off. Travel to next piece of apparatus.' During demonstrations the observers can be asked to 'Look out for and tell me about good, held positions and their levels. Look out for and tell me about interesting travelling you see at different levels.'

FINAL FLOOR ACTIVITY

This could be as simple as a group of four jumps on the spot, alternating with jumping or travelling forwards a short distance for four, then to one side for four, then back to starting place for four.

Year 2 • December • Lesson 4

LESSON PLAN • 30 MINUTES

Emphasis on: (a) jumping strongly and landing softly, absorbing shock; (b) rolling; (c) participating wholeheartedly in almost non-stop physical activity.

FLOORWORK · 12 minutes

Legs

(1) Do little jumps on the spot, stretching ankles strongly to push you. Keep your body straight, but let your knees bend to make the landings soft and quiet. Jump, land, bend.

(2) After a short run of about four strides, jump straight up, pushing up with one or both feet. Stretch body again in the air. Do a soft, squashy landing, with a good knee bend.

(3) Now swing both arms high above head to help your jump. When you land, show me how your arms stretched forwards or sideways can help your balanced, controlled landings.

Body

(1) Lie on your back, curled up small, then roll backwards and forwards from seat all the way to your shoulders and hands. Put your chin on your chest to keep your back rounded.

(2) Now lie on your back, curled up small, with hands clasped under knees. Roll from side to side. Try to roll to one side, then the other side, then right over on to your back again. 'Side to side... and right over.

(3) Lie on your back with body straight and arms by your sides. Keep straight and roll over on to your front, then back on to your back again. Pull across with the opposite shoulder or straight leg.

Arms

(1) Put both hands on the floor with arms straight and fingers pointing forwards. Now jump your feet off the floor, gradually bouncing up higher.

(2) Keep your head looking forwards. If you look back under your arms, everything will be upside down.

(3) Try three or four preparatory jumps. When you feel ready, give an extra strong push to take your shoulders above your hips and your hips above your hands.

APPARATUS WORK · 16 minutes

(1) Walk round the room, touching floor and mats only. You may run and jump on to or across mats, benches and low planks.

(2) When you land from your jump, try a squashy landing and a full knee bend that takes you right down on to your back. Finish by rolling sideways, spring up on to feet, and off you go again!

(3) Now step up on to apparatus. Jump off, keeping your body nicely stretched, and do a soft, quiet, squashy landing. If you like, add in a sideways roll again, then off to the next apparatus.

(4) Can you use a bunny jump action to bring you on to a piece of apparatus? Hands grip sides or are flat on top, then jump and pull or twist feet up on to apparatus. Leave with either a jump, or a roll off from a sitting, kneeling or lying position.

FINAL FLOOR ACTIVITY · 2 minutes

To a four count beat, can you make up a simple pattern of jumping in your own floor space? (For example, one foot to same; one foot to other; one foot to both; both feet to both.)

LESSON NOTES • 4 LESSONS DEVELOPMENT

FLOORWORK

Legs

(1) At start, talk about and look at good ankle actions. Because the ankle joint is seldom fully extended in everyday life, there will be many poor performances. The feeling is of the head pushing up and the toes pushing and pointing down.

(2) Emphasise 'Upward jump, not long jump' as they go higher because of the run up. Ankle and knee joints 'give' slowly on landing, to absorb shock and keep it quiet.

(3) Good arm action helps the lift-off, the balance in the air, the balance on landing, and the appearance of the performance.

Body

(1) We are used to travelling on feet, and on feet and hands, but not so used to travelling on other large body parts and surfaces. This long, slow rock from seat all the way to shoulders, with hands next to shoulders and thumbs in, needs to be practised and experienced. The move backwards is like the start of a backwards roll. The move forwards is like the end of a forward roll.

(2) Those who do not like rolling backwards and forwards do not usually mind the quite long travel of a sideways roll.

(3) The straight body sideways roll is a good rolling activity and a useful way to link two balances together.

Arms

(1) For the little bounces up and down hands are placed shoulder width apart under the shoulders, feet and knees together.

(2) Head is tilted back a little way to look ahead of where your hands are.

(3) Legs are kept well bent to shorten the lever. There will be several examples of well controlled performances in most classes. Use these to demonstrate.

APPARATUS WORK

(1) Short runs, with the emphasis on height in the jumping when there is plenty of space and you are completely unimpeded.

(2) With nine or ten mats available in a typical infant lesson, there will be continuous opportunities for the 'Run, jump, squashy landing and roll sideways.'

(3) A quick on to, and up and from the apparatus, to practise landing from a greater height, with or without the sideways roll.

(4) All pieces of apparatus can be arrived on by taking all the weight momentarily on the hands and doing the bunny jump action. They then travel to a point where it is possible to leave the apparatus either by a jump and a quiet landing, or by a roll.

FINAL FLOOR ACTIVITY

'Pattern' means a repeated series of actions. At least two actions are needed to make a series.

LESSON PLAN • 30 MINUTES

Emphasis on: (a) sequences and linking a series of actions, and showing the ability to remember and repeat them; (b) observing performances with interest, and making comments on what was done and what was liked.

FLOORWORK   12 minutes

Legs
(1) Can you do an upward jump where you are, then show me a very short run into another high jump?

(2) When you are in the air, can you stretch out your body from straight arms above head down to pointed ankles and toes?

(3) Be still for your start and after your finish each time. Always look for a good space to run into.

Body
(1) Show me a favourite, still body shape (e.g. stretched long or wide, curled, arched, twisted). Can you move on to a different body part and show me a new body shape?

(2) Make up a sequence that you can remember of three or four joined up and changing body shapes on different body parts.

(3) The linking movements will be particularly interesting to me. I will be looking for any new ideas that I can learn from (e.g. rolls, jumps, twists, lowering, rocking).

Arms
(1) All start ready in a crouch position, as for a bunny jump. Show me a pattern of ways you like to travel using hands and feet. Show me contrasting actions.

(2) Variety can include hands only, feet only; walk hands, then jump feet forwards; low crawl, high cartwheel; hands and feet wide, then close together as you travel.

(3) Different body parts can lead the movements and your body can have back, front or one side towards the floor.

APPARATUS WORK   16 minutes

(1) Show me a beautifully stretched body, standing tall on tiptoes in your own floor space. Jump on the spot, then travel up to and on to a piece of apparatus and show me a still body shape. Leave the apparatus and stop in a new floor space, nicely stretched again.

(2) Start in a space near apparatus. Make your hands important in travelling up to and on to your apparatus. On the apparatus, travel using hands, or hands and feet strongly. See if some of your floorwork travelling can be used. Leave with a high jump and a nice, 'giving' landing, followed by a sideways roll if you want.

(3) Starting at your number one apparatus places, try to do the following sequence for me: (a) start on the floor in your own space, do an upward jump on the spot, then travel up to and on to the apparatus; (b) show me a firm, still body shape as soon as you arrive on your apparatus, then travel using hands, or hands and feet strongly; (c) just before leaving the apparatus, can you show me a still body shape, different to your first one; (d) leave with a stretched upward jump or by rolling from the apparatus, and finish, still, in your own floor space.

FINAL FLOOR ACTIVITY   2 minutes

Show me a starting position with a firm, whole body shape. Run and jump, making that shape in the air. Change your starting shape and your shape in the air.

FLOORWORK

Legs
(1) Three actions to be linked together. Jump, run and jump. The 'very short' run, of about 3 or 4 metres only, takes you into the space you decided on during your jump on the spot.
(2) Twice, in the stationary and running jumps, there is an emphasis on stretching the whole body firmly to make it work as hard as possible and the actions look as good as possible.
(3) Infants like to be moving all the time and need to be encouraged to hold still at start and finish.

Body
(1) Arms, legs and spine work together to make the whole body shapes. The class should be showing shapes while standing, lying, kneeling, sitting, upended on shoulders, arched on back or front.
(2) Different body shapes on different body parts, all smoothly joined up, will be done in your own space with minimum travelling.

(3) Observers can be asked 'Watch the demonstrations carefully and tell me which group of shapes you like. Tell me also how the performer linked the shapes together.'

Arms
(1) Insist on slow, careful travelling, using actions that involve the whole body and put most of the weight on the hands.
(2) Ask them to put a name to their actions, to make them think about the nature of them. (For example, crawling, hands and feet moving together; stretching out and curling in as hands only go forwards, then feet catch up; bunny jumping forwards from feet to hands, then jump feet up to hands again; bouncing on all fours as long body springs up and down, moving forwards; cartwheels.)
(3) We usually travel with head leading and front of body towards the floor.

APPARATUS WORK

(1) We are trying to encourage them to make a short sequence with a beginning, middle and end. This middle is simple and short – make a still body shape after arriving on the apparatus.
(2) Varied travelling on hands and feet is still fresh in our memories from the floorwork. Now we practise and develop it on both floor and on apparatus, still looking for variety in actions and leading parts, and whole body involvement.
(3) If groups start at their number one apparatus places, i.e. the one they brought out, the numbers will be evenly shared around all pieces. On alternate weeks they move round clockwise and anti-clockwise, meeting at least three sets of apparatus each lesson. The eventual demonstrations will be of whole groups showing how well they share the apparatus and floor to work almost non-stop at their sequences. They include all the elements from the training in the floorwork, here expanded and developed on floor and apparatus.

FINAL FLOOR ACTIVITY

A triangle of three actions to bring you back to your starting place is recommended.

Year 2 • February • Lesson 6

LESSON PLAN • 30 MINUTES

Emphasis on: (a) balancing; (b) maintaining good body tension and posture.

FLOORWORK   12 minutes

Legs

(1) Stand tall, balanced on tiptoes. Run, jump and land in a beautifully balanced position where your body is supported on one or both legs in a way that is hard to hold steady.

(2) Go into your balanced finish slowly so that it becomes a landing changing into a balance, almost in slow motion.

(3) The difficulty comes from being on an unusual part of one or both feet, or holding your body in a difficult position.

Body

(1) Choose some part or parts of your body other than feet to balance on. Stretch those parts not being used for support to enhance the look of the balance.

(2) From your first balance, can you change to a new supporting part or parts by way of a simple linking movement (such as a roll, twist, spin, arch), still not on feet?

(3) Please show me your three balances nicely linked together with an interesting set of supporting parts and linking movements.

Arms

(1) Swing up on to your hands and try to hold a balance for two or three seconds. Make it a strong, safe position by keeping your arms straight and your head looking forwards.

(2) Try to let your swinging up leg go a long way past your head, while the kicking foot hardly leaves the floor. A long, straight line in your legs will help to balance you.

(3) 'Feel' how much or how little effort is needed to take you up on to your hands. Practise and your body will remember.

APPARATUS WORK   16 minutes

(1) As you visit each piece of apparatus, can you start off standing tall and still? Travel up to and on to the spparatus, and hold a still balance on any body part or parts. Spring up and off your apparatus with a beautifully stretched body in the air. Land in a nicely balanced position with a strong, firm body.

(2) Still move from apparatus to apparatus, but this time stay longer on each piece to include travelling actions that can link up balances on different parts of the body and apparatus. Balance, travel; balance, travel; balance, travel; then spring high up and off your apparatus to land, neatly balanced.

(3) Starting at your number one places, can you stay and practise to repeat, improve and remember the following: (a) start and finish on the floor in a firm, still, well balanced position; (b) travel up to, on to, and on your apparatus, including a variety of balances on different body and apparatus parts; (c) leave apparatus with a lively spring and a well balanced landing; and (d) have one more practice at the handstand just before your finish position.

FINAL FLOOR ACTIVITY   2 minutes

Show me the hardest balance on one or both feet that you can do without wobbling.

LESSON NOTES • 4 LESSONS DEVELOPMENT

FLOORWORK

Legs
(1) The starting position must be a challenge to hold steady right up on tiptoes. After landing, they either hold a position with knees slightly bent, on tiptoes, or they move to standing on one foot, the upper body or other leg in a position that makes balancing difficult.
(2) If you rush into a balance, you will almost certainly fail.
(3) Near horizontal standing on one foot, with whole body and other leg inclined forwards or to one side. Upstretched arms add to the difficulty and body tension, and improve the appearance.

Body
(1) They can use any body part or parts as long as there is a problem with being still. The problem is increased by the need to hold non-supporting parts stretched and firm.

(2) They have to plan how to move slowly to an adjacent body part to arrive in a new balance. Teacher commentary and many demonstrations will extend class repertoire of such difficult linking movements.
(3) Three is sufficiently challenging, but also short enough to be remembered, practised, repeated and improved.

Arms
(1) Long arms swinging from above head, or a short swing up of one leg behind you, are two controlled ways to take you on to your hands.
(2) A comparison with a tightrope walker's long, straight pole is recommended to encourage a long line through both legs.
(3) We are trying to develop body tension and the feeling of how much effort to apply.

APPARATUS WORK

(1) We start off with a short, simple sequence, emphasising good, firm body tension throughout. Show a still balance at start and finish, one balance only on the apparatus, and a good move into a balance after a landing from the apparatus.
(2) As in the balancing sequence in floorwork, they are now moving from balance to balance on apparatus, using travelling actions as linking movements.

(3) Over the four weeks of the lesson's development, the class will build up their repertoire, step by step, enabling them to include all the elements within the challenge they have been given. They should experience the variety of working on three different pieces of apparatus each lesson.

FINAL FLOOR ACTIVITY

Some will make balancing difficult by working on one foot and placing the other leg in most unusual positions. Others, working on one leg, will use the whole of the upper body, placing it in such difficult positions as tilted horizontally, from upstretched arms right down to stretched, non-supporting leg.

61

Year 2 • March • Lesson 7

LESSON PLAN • 30 MINUTES

Emphasis on: (a) partnerwork with its enjoyable and co-operative experiences; (b) working hard to achieve success.

FLOORWORK   12 minutes

Legs
(1) One partner practises and improves a simple, repeating floor pattern of walking, running, jumping or skipping in own floor space. The other partner practises a repeating pattern, using the whole floor space.
(2) One after the other, show your sequence twice through to your partner, who watches and remembers it.
(3) Can you now perform together, doing the on the spot pattern, then the sequence that uses the whole floor space?
Body
(1) From the same starting position, facing each other, can you very slowly build up a pattern of whole body movements, taking turns to decide the next one. I am looking for big body stretches (long and wide), curls, twists, arching.

(2) Remember to work slowly so that you can mirror each other. Do two, then repeat. Improve and remember them before going on to a third movement.
(3) Are you showing any variety (e.g. changing direction or level) or contrast (e.g. a sudden change of speed)?
Arms
(1) Follow your leader, travelling slowly on hands and feet, repeating your pattern of three or four varied actions.
(2) Leader, can you include a change of direction, not always travelling forwards?
(3) Other partner, you become the new leader now. Keep working at the same sequence. Can you change it slightly by making a different body part lead (e.g. not always the head)?

APPARATUS WORK   16 minutes

(1) One leading, one following, travel up to and on to each group of apparatus, then return to your starting place. Start again with the other partner leading, to see if he can remember exactly where you went and what you did.
(2) This time, as you follow each other on the apparatus, try to show me good support on hands and feet, with some interesting big body movements like you used together in the floorwork.

(3) Starting on the floor on opposite sides of your piece of apparatus, can you try the following: (a) in own space partner A demonstrates the leg activity pattern from the start of the floorwork; (b) partner B copies, then travels up to the apparatus, using one or more of the leg actions from the floorwork; (c) partner A copies the travel up to the apparatus; (d) slowly, agreeing who is leader, they pass each other, with an identical action; and (e) travel freely to finish in partner's starting position.

FINAL FLOOR ACTIVITY   2 minutes

Partner A leads a simple pattern of travelling along straight lines. Partner B leads a pattern of travelling along curving lines.

FLOORWORK

Legs

(1) They must be simple patterns, because they are to be remembered and performed, one after the other. However, to justify the name 'pattern', there must be at least two repeated actions.

(2) Each watches the other, once or twice through, then they perform one after the other, starting and finishing side by side.

(3) Now they 'follow the leader', facing each other for the routine on the spot, then travelling, one behind the other, using the whole room space.

Body

(1) One partner leads the sequence by showing the first body action. (For example, standing with arms and legs wide, like a star.) Other partner, now in the same wide stance, leads into the second movement. (For example, lower to sitting, curled tight, head on chest.) And so on, slowly, with much repetition of first position.

(2) You 'improve' by applying firm body tension to make the whole body shape look neat and under control. No slouching!

(3) For example, from the curled sitting they could lie down and roll sideways with a stretched body on to front. A sudden change of speed can happen at the very end of a stretch or curl.

Arms

(1) If the pair have their own little 'stage' to work on, not impeding others' floor space, a pattern of three or four ways to travel might take them in a triangle or rectangle back to own starting places.

(2) A change of direction happens when your side or your back is leading the travelling, rather than the more usual forward facing head.

(3) Bunny jumps, for example, can be used to travel sideways, with feet and hands zig-zagging along.

APPARATUS WORK

(1) If the travelling is kept really simple, the whole sequence can take place in instant unison, about 2 metres apart. Follower notes: What actions? How are body parts being used? What shapes are clear within the travelling? Are there any direction changes?

(2) The same activity, but with a longer stay on apparatus, giving time for examples of big stretching (wide and long), curling, twisting or arching movements within your travelling.

(3) Groups start at their number one apparatus places where they practise, improve and remember all the parts of their sequence. By providing good demonstrations, groups will be helped with ideas for their next piece of apparatus.

FINAL FLOOR ACTIVITY

Keep it simple enough to enable the follower to mirror the leader throughout. They change roles when the first leader stops and does an about turn as a signal to change over duties.

Year 2 • April • Lesson 8

LESSON PLAN • 30 MINUTES

Emphasis on: (a) awareness and good use of effort and speed to achieve a controlled performance – feeling how we move; (b) using contrasting movements for a more spectacular and polished performance.

FLOORWORK   12 minutes

Legs
(1) Travel in a variety of ways, using legs. Can you include actions that are small, light and gentle, and actions that are large, lively and strong?
(2) One way to organise it is to do the gentle actions in your own floor space, then the vigorous actions, travelling away from and back to your own space.
(3) Think about your actions and the ways that the feet and legs are working to make the actions 'feel' so different.

Body
(1) Show me a firm balance and work hard to show a clear body shape. Being balanced means that your body has to work hard not to wobble about.

(2) Contrast this strong position by relaxing and gently moving to another part or parts to balance strongly again. Work your body hard to show a firm, clear shape.
(3) Be strong, then relax, two or three times, as you plan your sequence of firm balances and contrasting linking actions.

Arms
(1) Travel using straight arms and legs slowly and strongly, with a lot of the weight on your hands.
(2) On all fours, can you experiment with hands and feet wide apart, then close together. Which is more difficult?
(3) From a standing start, pretend you are travelling side to side along a bench, gripping it with hands only. Let your soft landings contrast with the strong gripping and twisting.

APPARATUS WORK   16 minutes

(1) Travel freely all round the room, showing me easy, quiet leg actions that contrast with a strong, upward jump on to a mat. Gentle, firm. Easy, strong. Soft, explosive.
(2) Travel freely on all the apparatus. Can you contrast for me strong, firm balances, using your whole body well, and your easier travelling actions in between? Coming off, can you do a vigorous, upward jump, then a soft, 'giving' landing and gentle roll?

(3) Start at your number one apparatus places to practise, repeat, improve and remember the following: (a) start and finish on the floor, away from the apparatus; (b) as you travel up to and away from the apparatus, include a change of speed at some point (e.g. an explosive jump away from the apparatus at the end of the sequence); (c) alternate travelling and balancing on the apparatus, showing strong balances and some strong travelling with arms straight.

FINAL FLOOR ACTIVITY   2 minutes

Stand still but relaxed. Accelerate into an explosive, upward jump with an easy, gentle, quiet landing. Stand tall and relaxed. Repeat.

64

FLOORWORK

Legs

(1) Gentle, quiet, easy, small steps, skips and bounces. Vigorous, strong, bigger, louder galloping, running and jumping. Run with knees raising high, big bounces and long leaps from foot to foot.

(2) A focus on 'where' by everyone will lead to better sharing of the floor in this space consuming activity. They might even develop a little rhythm. On the spot, 3,4,5,6; travelling for 1... and 2... and 3... and 4... and 5... and home again!

(3) To be able to demonstrate ('Who will volunteer?'), they must know their actions and uses of the relevant body parts.

Body

(1) Ensure that they are balancing with difficulty and not just standing, kneeling or sitting easily.

(2) From 'feeling strong' in their firm balance, ask them to feel relaxed and easy as they transfer to another supporting body part, then firm up strongly again.

(3) An obvious contrast is in the use of levels, from highest position on tiptoes or one foot, down to being on one knee and one elbow, for example.

Arms

(1) On all fours, walking action; hands only, then feet only; front or back towards floor; hands walk, feet jump to astride hands; or cartwheels.

(2) Wide is difficult because arms are at an angle. Close is difficult because you need to be supple enough to bring feet near to hands, arching high.

(3) All weight on hands will happen more often now, e.g. for the vertical or lower than vertical cartwheels, or the swing of legs across while staying on hands.

APPARATUS WORK

(1) The quiet, easy actions will be slower than the accelerating sprint into the dynamic jump.

(2) On the apparatus, strong, still balances will alternate two or three times with travelling. At any one time, the hall should be full of still, strong, firm balances and travelling. If necessary, to reinforce the inclusion of balances, the teacher can call out 'Be still, those who are now balancing. The others, keep on travelling, and now... stop! Balancers, start your turn to travel now, keep going... and stop!'

(3) All the elements from the floorwork are now being asked for on both floor and apparatus. There will be contrasts of speed and effort, and different 'feelings' within the bodies of the performers at the different parts of their sequences.

FINAL FLOOR ACTIVITY

As they stand still and tall, their weight is slightly forwards on the balls of the feet, ready for the off. From stillness, they burst into acceleration for the jump, with its explosive drive up and off. A quiet landing nearly in slow motion, with knees and ankles 'giving' and often one foot landing after the other, provides contrasting leg activity.

Year 2 • May • Lesson 9

LESSON PLAN • 30 MINUTES

Emphasis on: (a) sequences and working harder for longer; (b) responding to set tasks with enthusiasm and confidence.

FLOORWORK   12 minutes

Legs

(1) Using your legs, show me a triangle of movements, starting and finishing at the same place. Can you include three different actions and be aware of your body shapes?

(2) Variety will come from your different actions and directions. Contrast can come from a change of speed or effort at some point. (An easy, slow, gentle action contrasts with a vigorous, accelerating one.)

(3) Legs can travel down at floor level, and lift up higher in shapes like a hurdler, star, tuck, jacknife, or a mixture (e.g. one leg straight down, the other bent back).

Body

(1) Practise back and forward, and side to side rolls from a curled up sitting position. When you go backwards and forwards, put your hands next to your shoulders and push forwards with them. Side to side, keep hands clasped under knees.

(2) Try to roll to one side, to other side, to first side and right over on to your back again. Side, side, side and over.

(3) Lie on your back with arms by your side. Twist by lifting one shoulder or leg to take you into a sideways roll, on to front and on to back again.

(4) Now, you choose. Start from a low crouch position; or sitting curled; or lying stretched, and plan a roll sequence to include at least two of the three we have practised.

Arms

(1) Slowly and quietly, show me two or more ways to travel on hands, or hands and feet, and see if you could give each action a name, as an introduction, if I asked you to demonstrate.

(2) Work in your own small floor space, and show me a still position to signal start and finish each time.

(3) Variety will come from a good mixture, such as high on hands, walking or cartwheeling; medium on strong, straight arms and legs, sometimes legs only, sometimes arms only; and low, crouched bunny jump actions on hands, with bent legs doing a variety of movements.

APPARATUS WORK   16 minutes

(1) Visit each set of apparatus in turn and show me a different method of travelling up to and on to each one for a very short time. Then travel away to a new floor space for your next, different travel.

(2) Continue to travel to the apparatus in different ways, but this time take all the weight on your hands to bring you on to the apparatus. A strong bunny jump grip and action should work at most pieces. Leave with a high jump, a squashy landing and, if there is space on your mat, try a roll.

(3) Starting at your number one apparatus places, can you practise, repeat, improve and remember a short sequences of your favourite activities on that apparatus and surrounding floor space?

FINAL FLOOR ACTIVITY   2 minutes

In a running sequence, can you include changes of direction, body shape and speed?

FLOORWORK

Legs
(1) Ask the class to walk round their little triangle with its 3 metre sides, starting and finishing on the same mark, line, floorboard (or whatever) each time. Walking might even be one of their three different actions.
(2) 'Different actions' infers greatly differing uses of feet and legs. (For example, easy passing each other as in walking; vigorous running into a leap; hopscotch; mixture of actions.)
(3) Asking for 'Low, middling and higher feet and legs actions' should inspire some varied ideas, worth demonstrating.

Body
(1) The 'Hands beside shoulders, thumbs in and fingers spread' is an important teaching point. In a backward roll, hands at shoulders push you on to feet. In a forward roll, hands push you forwards and up on to feet.
(2) In rolling sideways, a swing into the movement by the combined knees and clasped hands is essential for a lively action.

(3) Left shoulder or leg does the twisting pull to the right.
(4) For example, from a low crouch, lower to sitting, and rock backwards and forwards; roll side to side to side and over on to back; stretch out straight lying on back; roll to left, then to right; sit up curled, rock back on to shoulders and hands; push forwards strongly up on to feet and back to starting crouch position.

Arms
(1) For example 'I am crawling with straight arms and legs; then walking hands only forwards, and jumping feet up to hands; then I finish with a cartwheel.'
(2) If you are kicking feet up to go on to hands, always check that you have room behind, away from others or apparatus.
(3) Like direction changes, level changes provide an obvious and interesting contrast within a performance.

APPARATUS WORK

(1) The 'up to and away from' travelling is the main emphasis. The two different methods of travel can use feet, or feet and hands.
(2) 'Feel strong in your hands and arms as you lift, pull, twist, roll, lever, spring' on to apparatus. For variety there should be a strong leg action into the upward jump and landing, and an easy, slow roll on a mat.

(3) During this relatively free activity, the teacher will be able to assess how well the class work on and share the floor and apparatus space; how confident and competent they are in managing their bodies in a wide range of apparatus situations; and how enthusiastically and wholeheartedly they participate in their vigorous physical activity.

FINAL FLOOR ACTIVITY

Changing speed in their running will include running on the spot when their progress is impeded by others, plus slowing down and speeding up. Go backwards with great care, looking over one shoulder.

Year 2 • June • Lesson 10

LESSON PLAN • 30 MINUTES

Emphasis on: (a) partner work to provide enjoyable new learning and social experiences not possible on one's own; (b) extending movement understanding because you need to recognise your partner's movements and be able to repeat your own.

FLOORWORK 12 minutes

Legs
(1) Travel side by side or follow the leader, going from space to space. Plan and agree the three varied actions you will use, i.e. one easy and quiet, one with a direction change, and one that explodes into a vigorous movement.
(2) Start and finish standing still. After your third movement, go again when you see a big enough space for two of you.
(3) A mixture of leading and following, and side by side, would be very interesting (e.g. side by side, going sideways).

Body
(1) Start off, not on your feet, and curl up very small. Stretch part of your body to reach out into the space around you. Curl in tight to support yourself on a new body part.
(2) Stretch a different part of your body to a different place in the surrounding space. Curl in tight to your first supporting body part.
(3) Show each other your curls and stretches. Plan a way to do them together, with some contact between you on the two stretches. (They will need to adjust their starting positions and relationships to accommodate the stretches.)

Arms
(1) Partner A demonstrates a favourite way to travel on feet and hands, or to be supported on hands only. Partner B observes.
(2) Partner B repeats this first action, and adds on one of his or her favourites. Partner A watches.
(3) Partner A repeats the two actions, and adds on a third one. Partner B watches carefully.
(4) Partner B performs all three actions only or adds in a fourth and last action, with partner A's approval.

APPARATUS WORK 16 minutes

(1) Follow your leader, who travels a short distance on floor and apparatus then stops, to let you copy and catch up. I would like to see some of the varied actions we did on the floor earlier.
(2) On apparatus, I would like to see the new leader demonstrating ways to go from a tight curl to a full stretch with a body part reaching out into space. Partner, once again, will observe, then copy. Travel freely, from apparatus to apparatus.
(3) Starting at your number one apparatus places, plan and practise: (a) a still starting position on the floor, one behind the other; (b) follow the leader, travelling up to and on to apparatus, using hands strongly to support you, then hold a tight curled position next to each other. New leader takes over, leads slowly into a full stretch, and then travels on apparatus, using hands and feet; (c) same leader comes away from apparatus, using a different leg action to the one that took you on at start.

FINAL FLOOR ACTIVITY 2 minutes

Take it in turns to be leader. Jump on the spot, then run and jump to face a new direction.

FLOORWORK

Legs

(1) Travelling on a diagonal, one slightly behind the other, takes little space, and still lets one observe the other. Recommend all travel in a straight line, not anti-clockwise in a big circle, getting in one other's way, as so often happens in primary schools.

(2) 'Your movement is like a sentence, with a start and a finish each time, please.' (A 'sentence' of three words.)

(3) They can be very creative and include: one working on the spot, one circling; or parting and closing as they travel.

Body

(1) In the 'Stretching and curling sequence', the stretching parts are varied and reach out into different places in space. (Can be to front, side, rear, low, high.) To enable this, we change our starting positions.

(2) They can be asked to 'feel' strong and firm as they stretch out the whole body. (No sagging!) Then they 'feel' relaxed and gentle as they fold in to their contrasting curl.

(3) They can be back to back; side by side; side to back; or facing, as necessary, to permit the momentary contact in the stretches.

Arms

(1) 'One favourite way only' must be emphasised, and we want the new activity to be within the capability of the observer.

(2) The second action needs to be able to flow on from the first, without too much of a linking problem.

(3) As well as being easily linked, we want the next action to have something different about it to maintain the performers' and (later) observers' interest. 'Different' may be the change of level, direction, body shape, body part leading or towards floor, and actions of course.

(4) The three or four activities, all flowing one after the other, should take three or four lessons to decide and develop.

APPARATUS WORK

(1) Leader goes and stops while partner observes the actions and any changes of direction, shape or speed. Following partner catches up with leader and stops. Leader, alone, goes and stops.

(2) If space permits on a piece of apparatus, include two or three examples of curling, then stretching. On mats, this can include rolls into kneeling, lying or standing stretched. On mats, benches, planks or low box top, the curl can be crouched on two feet, lying on back, front or one side, on knees, upended on shoulder and hands. Follow these with the many possible stretchings out.

(3) The various floorwork activities are now requested, this time to be performed on floor and apparatus. Include: (a) two ways to travel between apparatus and starting/finishing place on floor; (b) taking whole body weight on hands, and travelling using hands and feet; (c) curling and stretching; (d) observing, copying and working in unison with a partner.

FINAL FLOOR ACTIVITY

On the 'jump to face a new direction', they can arrange to change over their roles as leader and follower.

Year 2 • July • Lesson 11

LESSON PLAN • 30 MINUTES

Emphasis on: (a) planning activities safely, and performing them with control; (b) practising wholeheartedly to improve, alone and with others; (c) reflecting and commenting on what they and others have done.

FLOORWORK   12 minutes

Legs

(1) Rise up on tiptoes with arms nicely stretched sideways for balance. Walk, then run a short distance to jump high and land facing a new direction. Let arms help balance.

(2) Each time, look for a clear space, and plan where you will go for your next jump. Never disturb others in the room.

(3) Changing direction is helped in the air if you swing into your jump with a strong arm or leg action. Or you can change direction on or after landing.

Body

(1) Make a bridge-like shape, standing with feet apart, body arched forwards, arms angled to the floor. Show me that you can make a different body shape. (For example, feet together, bend legs and back to go down to a curled shape.)

(2) Can you now change to a new bridge-like shape? (For example, sitting with bridge below knees.)

(3) In your own space, continue to change from a bridge to another shape, back to a bridge, then to another shape. A sequence of three of each would be pleasing.

Arms

(1) Show a partner your best way to take your body weight on your hands. Your partner will watch, then tell you what he or she particularly liked about your demonstration.

(2) Change over. Now the other partner shows a favourite way to take all the weight on to the hands. Once again, the watcher tells what was liked in the demonstration.

(3) You might like the neat, still, starting and finishing position; the good, safe, straight arms; the neat body shape, maybe with legs straight and together; or the nice high hips in a bunny jump. Say what you liked.

APPARATUS WORK   16 minutes

(1) Follow your partner, who will take you up to each piece of apparatus, show you a way to take weight on hands only on the apparatus, then move on to the next place. On and off quickly.

(2) Other partner now leads, and shows a short walk, a short run and a careful jump to land on a mat or to cross mat, bench, low plank or low box top. When you land you can try a squashy landing and a roll if you like. Following partner stays back, watching, until there is space to follow and copy.

(3) On your own now, start at your number one apparatus places to practise, repeat, improve and remember: (a) a still start and finish on the floor, away from apparatus; (b) travelling on to apparatus, using your arms strongly as you move along or support yourself; (c) within your travelling to see how often you can make a bridge-like shape on apparatus, or on apparatus and adjacent floor.

FINAL FLOOR ACTIVITY   2 minutes

Stand, balanced, on one or parts of both feet, with arms stretched. Walk a few steps and stop in a different balance on one or both feet.

FLOORWORK

Legs
(1) This activity needs a lot of whole body control and good body tension as you hold a balanced start; run and jump to land steady without a stumble or wobble; and organise your direction change.
(2) The runs must never be long because the run and jump are of equal importance. Some runs might only need two or three strides if the only space is nearby.
(3) A swing up with one arm or leg turns your body towards the other side, helpful often if you are approaching a wall.

Body
(1) The nature of a 'bridge-like shape' can be emphasised by asking the class to point out examples in the hall, to identify the arched shape.

(2) Bridges can be held standing with front, back or one side towards the floor; or upended on shoulders, head and hands.
(3) Variety comes from different supporting parts and different levels. (For example, high on feet; medium on one hand and one foot with one side towards floor; low on heels and shoulders, back towards floor.)

Arms
(1) All weight has to be supported on hands for a second or two. Many will do cartwheels and handstands. Others will do a bunny jump.
(2) Each can demonstrate two or three times to ensure at least one good one.
(3) 'Reflecting and evaluating' is a requirement within National Curriculum physical education. Working in pairs enables every pupil to practise it without the possible embarrassment of speaking to the whole class.

APPARATUS WORK

(1) Because this is a simple activity, they can follow quite close, one behind the other. 'On how many apparatus surfaces can you and your partner perform, with straight arms and bent legs in the next minute?'
(2) Leading partner is responsible for planning to go where both partners will have space to perform the approach, the jump, and the landing and roll.

(3) About five minutes are spent practising at each of the three sets of apparatus they will try to visit. This gives time to practise, repeat and improve their sequences. The emphasis is on strong arm support as you travel, alternating with stops at various places to demonstrate a still, bridge-like shape. The still, erect start and finish should be pursued as a way for the performer to signal 'I am ready to start' and 'I have completed my sequence'.

FINAL FLOOR ACTIVITY

If a still balance on one foot is beyond anyone's ability, tell them to place the toes of the other foot on the floor to help balance. The balances can be 'different' by holding non-supporting foot in different ways, or by inclining the upper body in different ways, e.g. horizontally forwards to side or back.

INDEX

apparatus 4–5, 7–8, 28, 30, 53, 59
assessing achievement 4
Attainment Target 4

balance 10–13, 18–19, 22–3, 26, 36–7, 40–2, 44–5, 60–1, 64–5, 70–1
body parts awareness 14, 29, 32–3, 48, 58, 60, 68
body shape 10, 14, 19–21, 24–7, 34–5, 48–50, 52–3, 58–9, 66, 70
body tension 21, 40, 53, 60, 63, 71
bridge-like shapes 11, 14, 18–19, 42–3, 54–5, 70–1
bunny jumping 16–17, 21, 26, 32–5, 38, 40, 56, 63, 66

cartwheels 30, 51, 53, 65–7
comments 41, 44, 58, 70

demonstrations 7, 9, 11, 14, 17, 19–21, 25, 27, 31, 34–7, 41, 43, 47, 49, 52, 55, 63, 65, 68, 71
directions 12–13, 36–7, 53–5, 63, 70
dynamics (effort, speed, force) 22, 64, 66–7, 69

follow the leader 8, 18–19, 24, 44–5, 62–3, 68, 70

good practice 4

handstand 46, 53–4, 66

jumping 6, 8, 10, 16–17, 20, 22–4, 30, 34–5, 38–9, 46, 50–2, 55–8

levels 12–13, 42–3, 54–5, 67, 71
linking movements 12, 20–1, 26, 29, 32–3, 35–6, 38–9, 42, 48–9, 52–4, 58–9, 60

National Curriculum 4

observation 18, 24–5, 33, 44–5, 47, 52, 58–9, 69

partner work 18, 24, 44–5, 62–3, 68–9, 70
pathways 43, 48, 55
pattern 23, 43, 54, 56–7, 62–3
performing 4, 10, 16, 26
planning 4, 9, 10, 13–16, 20, 23, 26, 28, 31, 33, 35, 37, 43, 47, 49–51, 70
Programme of Study 4

reflecting 4, 26, 70–1
responding to instructions 6–7, 9, 28–9, 35, 50–1, 66
rolling 10, 16–17, 26–7, 34, 38–9, 43, 46–7, 56–7, 66–7

safety 9, 13, 15, 17, 28–9, 31, 33, 35, 38, 41, 60
sequences 18, 20–1, 26–7, 31, 35, 38–40, 42–5, 47–9, 52–3, 58–9, 61–3, 66, 71
space awareness 12–13, 36, 45, 54–5
swinging as aid to movement 7, 17, 31, 46–7, 56, 60–1, 71

teacher commentary 13, 25, 29, 31, 51, 61
travelling 6–8, 10, 12–15, 24–6, 28, 30, 32–4, 36–7, 40–2, 44, 48, 50–2, 54, 57, 63–6, 68

variety and contrast 15, 22–3, 30, 32–3, 37, 41–2, 45, 48, 50, 52–3, 58, 62, 64–7, 71